INTRODUCTION TO RESEARCH IN PSYCHOPATHOLOGY

McGraw-Hill Paperback Series in Psychopathology

Norman Garmezy, *Consulting Editor*

Holzman: Psychoanalysis and Psychopathology

Maher: Introduction to Research in Psychopathology

Forthcoming Books in Series

Basowitz: Psychosomatic Disorders: Research and Theory

Becker: Manic-depressive Disorders: Research and Theory

Bibace, Kaplan and Wapner: Developmental Approaches to Psychopathology

Cohen: Biological Research and Theory in Psychopathology

Dahlstrom: Assessment of Psychopathological Behavior

Garmezy: Schizophrenia: Research and Theory

Goodrich: Disorders of Childhood: Research and Theory

Kalish and Geer: Learning Theory and Psychopathology

Parsons: Organic Disorders: Research and Theory

Rosenthal: Genetics of Psychopathology

Solomon, Kramer, and Wechsler: Social Psychological Approaches to Psychopathology: Research and Theory

Speisman: Neurotic Disorders: Research and Theory

Strupp: The Modification of Psychopathological Behavior

West: Experimental Induction of Psychopathological States

Brendan Maher

Riklis Professor of Behavioral Science and
Dean of the Graduate School, Brandeis University

Introduction to Research

in Psychopathology

McGraw-Hill Book Company

New York   St. Louis   San Francisco   London
Sydney   Toronto   Mexico   Panama

**INTRODUCTION TO RESEARCH
IN PSYCHOPATHOLOGY**

Library of Congress Catalog Card Number 71-85166

234567890 VBVB 76543210

*This book was set in Caledonia by Vail-Ballou
Press, Inc., and printed on permanent paper and
bound by Vail-Ballou Press, Inc. The designer was
Paula Tuerk; the drawings were done by J. & R.
Technical Services, Inc. The editors were Walter
Maytham and Timothy Yohn. Peter D. Guilmette
supervised the production.*

For Becky, Tom, Nicky, Liam, and Niall

Editor's Preface

This is the first volume of a series devoted exclusively to recent developments in abnormal psychology. In the original prospectus for the McGraw-Hill Paperback Series in Psychopathology, it was proposed that the project would have an explicit viewpoint:

> Its intent is to bring to the undergraduate student some sense of the excitement, the scope and the direction of research in abnormal psychology using the context of various theoretical formulations that have proved useful in integrating clinical and laboratory data. The Series will not ignore clinical content; rather, it shall place stress upon the interdependence of clinical observation and experimental findings. Hopefully too, the volumes shall provide the student with an awareness of methodological and technical difficulties, the complexities of controls and the breadth of the research problems that confront experimental psychopathologists today.

This was not always the direction of the abnormal psychology course. When William James published his monumental *Principles of Psychology* in 1890, he paid only fleeting attention to abnormal phenomena. Here and there he referred to alterations of consciousness in hysterics, to memory dysfunction in the aphasic and the amnesic, to insane delusions and hallucinatory imagery, to the "collecting instincts" of the kleptomaniac, to the tardiness of inhibition in imbeciles and dements, to the "explosive will" of the impulsively disordered in contrast to the "obstructed will" of the excessively inhibited, and to fear as an emotion of extraordinary power and pervasiveness. The substance of James's views bore the heavy mark of German psychiatry: "The delirium of fever, the altered self of insanity," he wrote, "are all due to foreign matters circulating through the brain, or to pathological changes in that organ's substance."

A half century earlier Wilhelm Griesinger, the leading psychiatric authority of his time, had proclaimed that mental diseases were diseases of the brain and that their causation was to be found in physiology and not psychology. But the turn of the century proved to be a period of ferment. Freud's great work, *The Interpretation of Dreams,* brought a new psychodynamic focus to the study of abnormality. In America, the roots of delinquency were being assigned to urban and familial pathology. Adolph Meyer, too, had begun to challenge neurophysiological speculations of mental disorder by urging a clear and unequivocal look at the patient's social environment as another source of his illness. Biology and psychology, asserted Meyer, were inseparable; brain and environment acted conjointly to produce maladaptation.

As our comprehension of the range of influences on mental disorder grew, the abnormal psychology course was slowly transformed. Inevitably popular with undergraduates, the initial structure of the course leaned heavily upon traditional psychiatric nosology embellished by exciting case histories that too frequently proved maximally titillating and minimally informative. The problem in organizing the course stemmed from the difficulty of integrating psychology's contributions with psychiatric thought. Moore's survey of 93 psychiatry texts published in the United States between 1861 and 1942 revealed only infrequent references to psychologists, with such illustrious names as Binet, Dunlap, James, Lange, McDougall, and Wundt leading all the rest. Apparently psychiatry was minimally beholden to psychology, and then primarily for concepts related to psychometrics, emotion, instinct, and the experimental tradition.

The full flowering of the contribution of psychology to an understanding of disordered mental processes has been of comparatively recent origin. The goal that Kraepelin, psychiatry's pioneering taxonomist, sought to achieve in Wundt's laboratory of creating an experimental psychopathology that would underlie the study of mental disorder is closer to fruition today than ever before. It would be foolhardy to suggest, however, either that experimental investigations are the sum and substance of abnormal psychology or that research has effectively solved the many problems of etiology, process, and treatment of the behavior disorders. Our hopes still lie with the future, but the direction now seems clear. At the turn of the twentieth century, Ziehen, on assuming the chair of psychiatry at Utrecht, converted the earlier narrow view of psychiatry that Griesinger had proposed. "A scientific psychiatry," he noted, "is not possible without a scientific psychology." The development of a scientific psychopathology must obviously make the same demands.

In this introductory volume to the many that will follow, Professor Brendan Maher, Riklis Professor of Behavioral Science at Brandeis University, has attempted to set out a panoply of research methods in abnormal psychology. His range is an extensive one, made necessary by what he perceives to be the challenge of psychopathology:

> For the psychopathologist, the paramount concern is to find answers to questions that have already been set by nature. What variables are responsible for the production of psychopathological phenomena, and what variables may be manipulated to change them? These are major questions and there is no guarantee that the answers will be discovered by the members of any single discipline.

To this end, Professor Maher has attempted to review some of the models and tactics of research in psychopathology, the nature of behavioral and biopsychological systems in abnormal processes, and the role played by genetic, epidemiologic, and developmental factors in disordered behavior.

Professor Maher is uniquely qualified for this challenging task. He has been trained in both England and the United States, has taught at Ohio State, Northwestern, Louisiana State, Harvard, Wisconsin, and Brandeis. His publications in psychopathology are many, and his text *Principles of Psychopathology* has met with an enthusiastic response from students, clinicians, researchers, and reviewers. His own research reveals a catholicity of interests that bodes well for one attempting a critical review of the research status of psychopathology. Brain function, conflict, language and thought disturbances in schizophrenia, autonomic and telemetric research, attitude measurement, and crime and delinquency have all come under his purview. The reader can take comfort in the fact that here is an author as broadly eclectic and yet as focused as the volume he has written. I hope that students will find his text a challenging one.

A final word of editorial appreciation to Miss Beverly Kaemmer is very much in order. Miss Kaemmer, as editorial associate of the series, has put her keen eye and adroit mind to the review of this and other manuscripts in the series in a way that has greatly facilitated the editor's task. She deserves and hereby receives the collective gratitude of the editor and the authors.

Norman Garmezy

Preface

For some years now, the study of abnormal psychology has been moving from its previous emphasis upon the individual case history and psychodynamics toward a more quantitative biopsychological base. Although this movement is comparatively recent, there is of course a long history of scientific research in psychopathology, and contemporary developments are best understood as the consequences of this tradition. That these developments have been long in coming is due, in large part, to the slow growth of the behavioral sciences: the vacuum that has existed has been filled, understandably, by a mixture of conjecture and conviction that continues to characterize much writing in psychopathology to the present day.

However, dramatic achievements in the fields of microbiology and genetics, in the neurophysiology of consciousness, in the application of the principles of learning to problems of therapy, in the refinement of epidemiologic techniques, in psychopharmacology, and in many other areas have changed the countenance of many of the classic problems of abnormal psychology. The research literature has expanded at an extraordinary rate and with it the need for the student to comprehend the concepts and terms with which it is written. Additionally he must be equipped with a reasonable grasp of the methods and tactics of behavioral research generally and their limitations when applied to particular problems.

It is to meet this need that this book was written. Used in conjunction with a basic textbook in abnormal psychology, it may serve to provide a background from which the student may proceed to reading the research literature with reasonable sophistication. It is the writer's hope that it may also stimulate the student to seek a balance between clinical and research emphases in his studies and thereby deepen his appreciation of the values of both approaches.

Expressions of gratitude are due to many colleagues and students who assisted in the preparation of this book. First of all, particular recognition is due to Norman Garmezy, whose editorial advice was invaluable at all stages of writing. Critical reading was provided by Irving Gottesman, Oscar Parsons, and Melvin Zax. Many of the matters dealt with arose from discussions with students at the University of Wisconsin, Brandeis University, and the University of Copenhagen. I should like to record my thanks to Professor E. Tranekjaer Rasmussen of the Psychological Laboratory at the University of Copenhagen and to his colleagues for the provision of facilities, assistance, and good company during the writing of the first manuscript. Secretarial help was given by Hanne Nielsen, Norma Skemp, Ina Moses, and Leslie Herman.

Brendan Maher

Contents

CHAPTER 1

THE LANGUAGE OF
PSYCHOPATHOLOGICAL
RESEARCH

We shall begin our study of research methods in abnormal psychology by examining in some detail a classic investigation in the field of psychosomatic medicine. A natural sequence of steps occurred in this investigation: the development of the ideas or hypotheses to be examined, the design of the research procedures, and the interpretation of the results that were obtained. This sequence can be detected in almost all systematic research and will provide a convenient framework for organizing our discussion here.

An Investigation of the Causes of Duodenal Ulcers

Some years ago a group of researchers (Weiner, Thaler, Reiser, & Mirsky, 1957) began to tackle the problem of the causes (or *etiology*) of duodenal ulcers. In general there had been two emphases in the study of this problem. One school of thought had focused upon biological or organic origins of the ulcer while another had been most interested in psychological explanations. The duodenal ulcer is, of course, an organic disorder. It consists of an inflammation of the lining of the duodenum, and internal bleeding may ensue: if untreated, the condition may be dangerous.

THE DEVELOPMENT OF A GENERAL HYPOTHESIS

Certain facts were available to the investigators. One of these was that in patients known to be suffering from duodenal ulcer the concentration of the substance *pepsinogen* in the blood is generally much higher than is found in people not suffering from ulcers. To be precise, 87 percent of ulcer patients had pepsinogen counts higher than the average count for non-ulcer patients. This fact, however, had more than one possible interpretation. It might be that the ulcer generates the high pepsinogen count and thus the fact does not really throw any light on the causes of the ulcer itself. However, an additional fact is that the high pepsinogen count is found to persist in the ulcer patient even after the ulcer has been completely healed. This latter observation suggests that (1) the pepsinogen count does not depend upon the existence of an ulcer and (2) a high pepsinogen count alone is insufficient to produce an ulcer. If it were sufficient, we should expect that the healed ulcer would keep recurring or that healing would be essentially impossible.

Although this train of deduction may seem plausible, it leaves many gaps to be filled. It seems reasonable to suppose that if high pepsinogen is present, both during and after the occurrence of the ulcer, it was also present before the ulcer developed. This may be reasonable but not by any means certain. It is always possible that the ulcer developed, that it altered pepsinogen production as a kind of by-product of its activity, and that this alteration was then irreversible, persisting long after the ulcer disappeared. Thus the proposition that high pepsinogen is a precursor of ulcer development remains as a *hypothesis* at this stage of our reasoning.

In the light of the facts available, the hypothesis has to take the form that high pepsinogen predisposes to ulcers but that it alone is not sufficient to produce them. Some additional cause must be found. At this point, the investigators turned to an entirely different source of information—specifically the data on psychological explanations of ulcer formation. From that direction there was available a body of clinical observations that had been made mainly by psychoanalysts. Their hypotheses might be summed up by stating that patients with duodenal ulcer seemed to have in common a conflict related to the persistence of strong infantile wishes to be loved and cared for, on the one hand, and to the unacceptability of these wishes to the patient's perception of himself as a mature adult. Such a conflict, it was suggested, was responsible for initiating a series of physiological processes that culminated in an ulcer. Yet, as one of the leading psychoanalytic investigators had observed, this kind of psychological conflict could be found in people who did not have ulcers. Thus, while the conflict seemed to be an important cause, it was not sufficient in and of itself to produce the ulcer. Here again there is also the possibility that the development of the ulcer places the patient in such a position of dependency on others (as many long-persisting illnesses do) that the psychological conflict is, perhaps, a consequence of the ulcer and not a cause.

Two sets of facts were now available to the researchers, one from organic studies and the other from clinical-psychological observations. To these they added a third observation—namely, that in most cases of duodenal ulcer there seemed to be a specific precipitating event. These events seemed to have no common feature that could be objectively described, and thus the investigators concluded that their common feature must be their psychological meaning to the individual patients. For example, one patient might develop ulcers after a divorce because this meant loss of love and care by a spouse; another might develop an ulcer after being promoted in his job because this meant added unwelcome adult responsibilities. The divorce and the promotion would have little obviously in common to an observer but would share the psychological characteristic that they both trigger the conflict of need for care and love versus pressure of adult responsibilities.

Armed with three kinds of data, Weiner and his colleagues were now able to formulate a general hypothesis about the etiology of duodenal ulcer. Their hypothesis read as follows: "A duodenal ulcer should develop when an individual with a sustained rate of gastric hypersecretion and the aforementioned psychic conflict is exposed to an environment that mobilizes conflict and induces psychic tension [p. 2]." This is a *general* hypothesis. Before the actual research can begin, it must be translated into a specific hypothesis, as the following paragraphs will show.

THE CONDUCT OF THE RESEARCH

The general hypothesis included three *variables* or factors. One of these was described as *gastric hypersecretion*. This general description must be turned into a definite value or magnitude of secretion. In this investigation the people to be studied were 2,073 Army draftees, and from each man a blood sample was taken for analysis. Pepsinogen counts were obtained from the blood samples. Two groups of soldiers were then selected: these consisted of 63 with the highest count (the hypersecretors) and the 57 with the lowest count (undersecretors). Thus we see that the factor of hypersecretion has now been defined in practice as meaning approximately the top 3 percent of pepsinogen counts in a large normal sample of adult males between the ages of seventeen and thirty.

By selecting Army draftees, the *factor* of *an environment that mobilizes conflict and induces psychic tension* has been defined in practice as undergoing army basic training. We should note here that the investigators have actually departed from their own previous thinking about the problem of environmental stress. Earlier they had concluded that the kind of stress that precipitates the ulcer would vary objectively from one person to another: by selecting subjects all of whom are going into the same objective stress—army training—they run the risk that it will be psychologically significant to only a few of their hypersecretors.

Their third factor, *the aforementioned psychic conflict,* presented them with a difficult problem of definition. Evidence of such a conflict can be obtained only indirectly. It was decided to use a battery of three projective measures of personality—the Rorschach test, the Blacky pictures, and the Draw-a-Person test. By interpreting the responses to these tests, it was possible to establish a definition of psychic conflict between masculinity and dependency. In fact, projective measures indicated that this conflict was present in the majority of hypersecretors anyway, although only nine of the hypersecretors actually developed an ulcer during basic training. No criterion measure could be found afterward to distinguish between the hypersecretors who developed ulcers and those who did not.

The investigators concluded that their basic hypothesis had been supported and that the reason only nine persons succumbed to the situation was, presumably, that army training was a psychologically significant stress for only this small number of potential victims.

At first glance the logic of events in this research investigation may appear to be straightforward and simple. The logic of the design is clear, the deductive processes are lucid, and the conclusions more or less obvious. However, as we progress in this book, we shall see that the conduct of this research illustrates the operation of certain basic principles. These principles fall under two general headings. One set of principles is derived from scientific psychology, both behavioral and biological. The second set of principles comes from the philosophy of science and relates to scientific method on the one hand and technological procedures on the other.

This book represents an attempt to provide the necessary information in a relatively condensed form, using examples drawn from research in abnormal psychology (or *psychopathology*) wherever these are available and suitable. For the psychopathologist, the paramount concern is to find answers to questions already set by nature. What variables are responsible for the production of psychopathological phenomena and what variables may be manipulated to change them? These are the major questions, and there is no guarantee that the answers will be discovered by the members of any single discipline, at least in the sense that disciplines are organized into separate departments in universities. Consequently, the serious psychopathologist is willing—indeed finds it necessary—to turn to any branch of science that holds promise of giving assistance. Thus concepts, methods, and techniques are borrowed from many fields, some of which normally lie outside the behavioral sciences as such. Anthropology, biochemistry, biology, genetics, physiology, and sociology are among the major contributors, but the limits of interdisciplinary cooperation may well extend beyond this as time goes on.

Psychopathology is an applied field of study. However, the psychopathologist, unlike the clinician, is concerned with the *discovery* and *formulation of laws* that will have effective application to distressed human beings. Skillful use of the technology may be appropriately regarded as the province of the clinician.

Psychopathology: Definitions and Concepts

We may now turn to definitions, proceeding from these to a consideration of the concepts that are currently used to study the problems of the field.

PSYCHOPATHOLOGY

Psychopathology may be defined as *the scientific study of disordered behavior*. As with most definitions, the terms of this one warrant some further explanation. By *scientific* is meant here that the psychopathologist adheres to certain standards in planning and conducting his investigation. While detailed analysis of these standards will be deferred to a later chapter, they may be summarized briefly here.

First, the scientist deals with data obtained by observations made under conditions of some *control*. The degree of control he can exercise will depend to a large extent upon the nature of the data being collected. In the study with which we opened this chapter, the degree of stress involved in army basic training was left to chance. For some draftees a fortuitous assignment to a tolerant noncommissioned officer, acceptable comrades, etc., might have operated to reduce stress. For other draftees the opposite state of affairs might have prevailed. Whatever happened was not under the control of the experimenters; the only degree of control they had was the gross fact that the subjects were all in the Army. Maximum control is achieved, generally speaking, by use of the *experiment,* but it should be understood that this is only one of the methods available to science and is not always possible nor the most appropriate. Where the scientist cannot produce experimental control, i.e., by manipulating the conditions under which his data will be obtained, he will seek to measure as many of the uncontrollable surrounding conditions as he can in order that he may estimate their effect upon his observations.

A concern with *measurement,* or *quantification* of some kind, is the second distinguishing characteristic of the scientist. In its simplest form quantification might consist of merely "present" versus "absent" or "did happen" versus "didn't happen." As the development of a particular science progresses, we find an increasing sophistication in the methods of measurement and in the precision with which they are made. Among the crucial features of scientific measurement is the accessibility of the method of measurement to other observers. If the method is properly defined and uniformly applied by other investigators, then when faced with the same event they will all report the same measured result. When there are discrepancies, they will be due to the observer's error rather than to any intrinsic unreliability of the measurement procedure itself. Thus, a parallel aspect of quantification is *observer agreement*—the power of the measurement method to produce agreement among independent observers.

Finally, we may note that the scientist is concerned with the *establishment of laws.* Laws describe the systematic relationships between regularly occurring events, and if there were to be such a thing as a unique event, it would, by definition, be beyond the scope of scientific investigation. As we shall see later, the concept of a "unique event" is debatable, although it has provided a basis for some early disputes in the psychology of personality. However, the psychopathologist may safely dismiss the issue as irrelevant to his purpose of establishing behavioral laws.

DISORDERED BEHAVIOR

Returning to our opening definition, we may now consider the meaning of the phrase "disordered behavior." Behavior may be described as *disordered, deviant, abnormal,* or *pathological* by reference to any of several common criteria. These criteria are applied separately or together under various circumstances. Let us consider some of the major criteria.

Personal distress.   We may use statements of distress made by an individual about himself as the basis for defining psychopathology. Thus, if a person complains of feeling continual tension or anxiety without apparent cause or describes himself as being frequently depressed and worried, then he will be of interest to psychopathologists even though the rest of his behavior may not be unusually different from that of people who do not make these complaints. In practice, complaints of this kind are generally accompanied by some behavioral deviations—for example, sleeplessness and loss of appetite—but these latter may not be of a magnitude to justify the term "pathological" when considered apart from the verbal complaints.

Disabling behavior tendencies.   Behavior that handicaps the individual in his everyday life is the second criterion for a definition of disordered behavior. Classic examples of this would be compulsions, such as frequent ritual hand washing, phobias, addictions to narcotics, and hysterical amnesias. In each case, the overt behavior symptom notably reduces the individual's daily efficiency. Generally, but not always, it is accompanied by feelings of distress. We regard these behavior patterns as pathological largely because they occur in situations in which more nearly adequate and less extreme responses are realistically possible. For example, we do not regard fear of poisonous snakes as pathological when it leads someone to be very cautious in snake-infested country; we would regard it as pathological if the same person were to show signs of panic when reading the word "snake" in a book.

Poor reality contact.   Although these kinds of behavior may be disabling, the psychopathologist would not regard them as lacking contact with reality. Poor reality contact is a term reserved for behavior marked by more extreme deviation from the norm and in which there is a perceptible lack of integration between the person's responses and the surrounding environment. Examples of this would include talking, smiling, and responding conversationally in an empty room; eating stones and dirt; appearing naked in public; developing complicated plans to foil "spies"; and confusion about one's own identity, spatial location, or orientation in time. Although the distinction is far from precise, it is usual to refer to behavior of this latter kind as *psychotic*, while that described in the preceding paragraph is termed *neurotic*.

Psychosomatic disorders. Psychopathologists have also been concerned with a class of human problems in which the prime focus of complaint is a bodily disorder—generally involving malfunction of the visceral nervous system. Peptic ulcers, hypertension, colitis, and asthma are among the major disorders in this group. They become of interest to the psychopathologist when they are determined, at least in part, by psychological factors as well as by biological dispositions in the patient. Psychological factors are not always evident in every case, but when they are, they are more akin to neurotic than to psychotic determinants.

Conduct disorders. Some individuals exhibit behavior that is antisocial or criminal and yet are apparently free from anxiety, never seek psychological help because of any sense of personal distress, and do not demonstrate lack of reality contact in the usual sense. These behavior patterns include overtly criminal activities, addictions to narcotics, exploitative use of others, and the like. Prison populations include numbers of this kind of person in addition to those found in mental hospitals. Some psychopathologists have argued that this behavior is truly psychotic, i.e., freed from reality controls; all psychopathologists regard it as deviant and a proper subject for their study.

When we reflect on these criteria, we notice that the term "behavior" has been applied rather widely. It has been used to include verbal behavior (complaints), motor movements (as in phobic avoidances), visceral or other inner bodily responses, and, by implication, conscious states inferred from statements of "feeling." There are reasons for this. The psychopathologist focuses upon any response that can be measured, or at least observed, and related to psychopathology. In doing so, he may use techniques and instruments that are also found in the hands of other scientists—physiologists, biochemists, geneticists, sociologists, and so forth. He does so not because of any intrinsic interest in the problems of these scientific disciplines but because of an overriding interest in arriving at valid solutions to the practical problems of psychopathology. Thus, he is generally uninterested in the responses of individuals who suffer from a purely bodily disorder in which no psychological malfunctioning is implicated. His interest in the genetics of schizophrenia is based upon an interest in schizophrenia: he may be unconcerned with the problems of genetic theory for their own sake. The important point is that he does not confine himself to the use of concepts and techniques that are primarily psychological unless these seem to offer the probability of providing a complete answer to the psychopathological problem in which he is interested.

Some Patterns of Psychopathology

PSYCHOTIC PATTERNS

Psychopathologists make a broad distinction between *neurotic* and *psychotic* patterns of disordered behavior. Clear differentiation between these two terms is still lacking, but the major points of difference may be noted. The essence of the distinction lies in the concept of *reality contact*. An individual is said to be in poor reality contact when his behavior—motor, verbal, or cognitive—appears to be unrelated to the environmental determinants that control the same behavior in the majority of people. Psychotic patterns thus include a variety of anomalies of which the following are the most prominent.

Sensory-perceptual anomalies. Responses may be made to stimuli that are not present to other observers. A patient may conduct a conversation in an empty room; he may complain of bodily sensations that appear to have no possible normal stimulus, such as being "eaten alive by snakes crawling under the skin"; he may complain of visual anomalies, such as the lack of depth perception ("the world all appears flat and made of cardboard").

Disorientation as to person, place, or time. Operationally defined, this refers to the individual's inability to remember his name, to know where he is, or to know the time, date, etc. He may be unable to recall these or may make erroneous identifications, believing himself to be somebody else.

Thought disorder. Individuals sometimes show disturbances in language and thought. These disturbances may be divided into two classes. They may involve no grammatical errors but may reflect instead a deficiency in inference from external events. Thus, a psychotic individual may state, "I am being constantly hounded by spies disguised as mailmen," in perfect grammatical style, but he draws an inference about mailmen that few observers could accept as valid.

A second class of language/ thought disturbance occurs when an inmate has difficulty in presenting a comprehensible sequence of language to express a thought. Associations of various kinds intrude, producing disorganized speech so that when trying to state "I saw my father and son" a hospital patient actually said, "I saw my father, son and Holy Ghost [Bleuler, 1950, p. 26]."

Motor anomalies. A fourth aspect of psychotic behavior is the frequent presence of bizarre modes of motor behavior. Prolonged holding of a fixed position such as standing for several hours on one leg is a marked feature of certain schizophrenic syndromes. Repeated gestures and bizarre motor mannerisms are also found.

Bizarre asocial behavior. Marked loss of awareness of the social unacceptability of some kinds of behavior would also lead to a classification of psychosis. Walking naked down a public street, smearing of excrement, and deterioration of grooming and personal appearance would be instances of this.

Prolonged extremities of mood. When an individual exhibits prolonged and extreme moods of depression or euphoria with the relevant accompanying behavior, he will generally be classified as psychotic. Thus an appropriate illustration would be a patient who has spent three years accusing himself of a minor peculation in business, his accusations being combined with severe self-mutilation and bouts of weeping lasting several hours at a time.

NEUROTIC PATTERNS

Neurotic patterns of behavior are generally regarded as derivatives of some relatively persistent anxiety. Some psychopathologists believe anxiety is, in turn, the consequence of a fundamental conflict of motives in an important area of the individual's life. Although neurotic patterns may share this common core, the kinds of symptoms identified as neurotic take many forms. Among the more typical patterns are:

1. Overt anxiety, apprehension, and dread
2. Somatic symptoms of fatigue, sleeplessness, loss of appetite, etc.
3. Ritualistic repetitive sequences of behavior, obsessions, and compulsions
4. Quasi-somatic complaints, such as anesthesias, paralyses, sensory deficiencies with no clear organic origin; defects of recall and of perception

In addition to the belief that these patterns represent the development of anxiety and avoidance responses is the accompanying view that they are best understood as the result of environmental influences with a relatively negligible contribution from genetic or biological factors.

The distinction between psychosis and neurosis implies a dichotomy, at least at the semantic level. Many psychopathologists do not, however, regard these as separate categories but as disorders possessing many similarities. By the same token, several attempts have been made to discover single dimensions underlying the various neurotic or psychotic syndromes. By way of illustration we might look at one of these, the concept of an *efficiency dimension*.

A GENERAL DIMENSION: EFFICIENCY

Wishner (1955) has suggested that the degree of severity or intensity of any condition of psychopathology might be scaled on a single dimension of efficiency. Efficiency in a mechanical system is inversely related to the amount of energy dissipated in nonproductive work, i.e., overcoming friction, etc. Much the same kind of analysis has been applied by Wishner to the behavior of individuals wherein the behavior can be seen as *focused* (i.e., contributing to the task at hand) or *diffuse* (irrelevant to the goals of the individual's effort). Efficiency may then be computed as some function of the ratio of focused to diffuse behavior, the severity of psychopathology being characterized by lower efficiency. Since this may be applied to any individual classified as normal, neurotic, or psychotic, it permits the establishment of a single dimension for the scaling of a variety of psychopathological categories. Application of this concept to the differences in efficiency between normal and schizophrenic subjects is to be seen in a study by Peastrel (1961). Subjects were conditioned to give a galvanic skin response (GSR) to a word. They were instructed to attend specifically to the meanings of the stim-

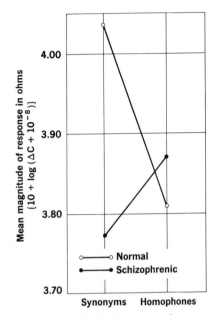

Fig. 1-1 *Differential effects of generalization to homophones and to synonyms in schizophrenic and control subjects. (Peastrel, 1961)*

ulus words. Generalization to synonyms and homophones was then tested, adequate attention to the meaning of the words being expected to lead to generalization to synonyms (wherein the meaning is the same as that of the original training word) but not to homophones (wherein the sound is the same but the meaning differs). Thus, a subject conditioned to the word CENT should generalize to PENNY but not to SCENT. Generalized responses to the homophone are irrelevant to the task instructions here and are thus diffuse in Wishner's use of the term. Peastrel's data are shown in Figure 1-1. The greater diffuseness of the psychopathological sample is clear from the data. Although these data might be interpreted in other theoretical terms, they are relevant here as an illustration of the application of the efficiency concept.

A fuller discussion of the validity of diagnostic categories will follow in the next chapter and need not be pursued further at this point. Before we can consider this and other research issues, however, we must extend our study of definitional matters to include some of the common terminology of the research scientist.

Research: Definitions and Concepts

There are many different ways in which research may be conducted, and a variety of tactics are available to the psychopathologist. However, underlying all of them is a common core of terms and definitions to which we can now turn.

Variable. A variable is any factor, event, or phenomenon that may assume different values, i.e., that may have *variable magnitudes.* Environmental factors such as heat, light, and sound; physiological factors such as fatigue and somatic injury; and psychological factors such as past learning and attitudes are all possible variables in research studies. When a specific factor did not vary or was prevented from varying in a study, we may say that it was not a variable in the study concerned. If a factor did vary but can be shown to have had no influence on the results of an experiment, then it was not a variable in the outcome. A distinction is made between *independent* and *dependent* variables and is described later in this chapter.

Hypothesis. Most, but not all, research begins with the formulation of a hypothesis to be tested. In essence the hypothesis states that a systematic relation will be observed to exist between two or more events. The hypothesis may be derived from a preexisting and explicit theory; it may have occurred as a hunch, leaving the investigator hard put to explain how he derived it; or it may simply state that a relationship already observed empirically will hold good for future observations. In the study of duodenal ulcer, for example, we see a hypothesis partly derived from empirical observation and partly from psychoanalytic theory. Although the derivation of a hypothesis may not always be clear, the statement of the hypothesis itself must be couched in explicit terms. Examples of the ways in which hypotheses are generated might be cited as follows.

Theoretical derivation. From the theory that schizophrenic deficit is due to a pathology of attention, we hypothesize that factors that improve attentional focusing will lead to an improvement in behavior when applied to schizophrenics. An example of this is to be found in the well-known study of Tizard and Venables (1957).

Intuitive derivation. Some paranoid patients believe that they are Christ. What would happen, you may ask, if several such patients were compelled to confront each other—would the logical impossibility of the situation lead to a behavior change? Such a study was performed by Milton Rokeach and reported in his book *The Three Christs of Ypsilanti* (1964). Here there is no clearly formulated theory of the effect of an empirical contradiction upon a false belief but a relatively intuitive estimate that something of interest must happen.

Empirical derivation. An empirically derived hypothesis might state that the investigator has noticed that the parents of schizophrenic patients appear to be unusually cold or aloof. He wonders whether this informal observation will be confirmed when made on a large sample under conditions of careful control.

Whatever the origin of a hypothesis, it must be stated in a testable manner before it can be researched. To be testable, the hypothesis must make clear the kinds of data that would support it and the kinds of data that would contradict it. For example, if we hypothesize that all frustration leads to aggression, then we must specify exactly what is meant by "frustration" and "aggression." When this is done, we can decide whether aggression did indeed occur or whether some other kind of behavior was elicited.

Law. When a specific hypothesis has been confirmed repeatedly, then its status will change to that of a *law*. A law is a formulation of the relationship between two or more sets of events that has been observed so often that there is no reasonable room to doubt that it is reliable.

Laws are often stated in mathematical terms, the numbers expressing the extent of the relationship or the number of factors that enter into it. Laws are statements of reliable empirical observations and thus may be subject to more than one theoretical interpretation. As a science progresses, it is usual for theories to be modified or abandoned in favor of new and more comprehensive ones. When this happens, the laws incorporated into the original theory are not changed; they may be restated as instances of a new and more general law, but they are not disconfirmed. It is quite possible to have sets of laws about events without having any theory to account for the relationship which the laws describe.

Theory. Within the field of psychopathology the meaning of the term "theory" is relatively unambiguous. A *theory* consists of a number of statements describing processes or relational structures that are *assumed* to account for observed laws and well-confirmed hypotheses. For a theory to be other than an organized tabulation of known facts it must involve assumptions that in some respect go beyond the available data. Thus, theory may refer to potentially measurable processes that have not yet been tested. Theories of psychopathology are almost exclusively couched in terms of real, but as yet unobserved, processes rather than in mathematical terms. Thus theories of neuroticism that proceed from observed relationships between personality and conditioning to inferences about constructs of "introversion" and "extraversion" may proceed to concepts of excitation and inhibition in the central nervous system. Such a progression is to be seen in the theoretical formulations of Eysenck (1957). Inasmuch as the excitability of neurons is potentially measurable, that is to say, that the terms "neuron" and "excite" have agreed definitions in the physical and electrical sense, then the theoretical use of these concepts implies real events happening in the nervous system but not yet directly observed. Presumably at some future time a measuring technique might be devised that would permit direct observation. However, until that is possible, the chief tests of the theory consist of the deduction of hypotheses that can be tested at some other behavioral or grossly physiological level.

Models. It is possible for a theory to be stated in terms that are sufficiently abstract so that several different sets of processes might be assumed to account for the empirical data, all the processes being compatible with the theory. Although the proper discussion of an example of this would be beyond the scope of this chapter, we might consider briefly the observation that decision time in a choice conflict increases as a function of the number of choices available. This observation has been made in specific circumstances, and many possible instances of the phenomenon have not actually been observed; e.g., nobody has yet reported a study of decision times when there are 100 alternatives from which to choose. However, from the observations available we might theorize that decision times increase with alternatives in linear fashion, i.e., that the decision time with 100 alternatives is ten times longer than with 10 alternatives. Accepting this for the moment, we might attempt to translate this into concrete terms by assuming that decision time is based upon the time it takes to scan each alternative visually. Or we might conclude that decision time is based upon the probability that a random choice will secure the "best" alternative; or that wide ranges of choice generate anxiety, and anxiety inhibits decision-making responses; and so on. Each of these formulations is initially compatible with the theoretical mathematics of the original statement. It is not possible to prefer one of these over the other without further research. They are just tentative approximations of the theory for investigation purposes and are generally referred to as theoretical *models*. Although there is some dispute about definition, most philosophers draw a distinction between a model and a theory along the lines indicated here. Achinstein (1965) has suggested four attributes of scientific models as follows:

1. A model consists of a set of *assumptions* about some object or system. These assumptions specify some of the attributes of the system or object under scrutiny in relatively concrete terms. For example, the Crick-Watson model of DNA molecular structure assumes that the constituents of the molecule are assembled according to a particular identifiable spatial arrangement.

2. A model includes not only sets of assumptions but puts them in such a way that they imply properties of the system that will in turn allow the *derivation of additional properties*. When we refer to the "billiard-ball" model of the molecular composition of gases, we note that its formal assumptions will permit the deduction of additional properties. The formal assumptions of this model can be paraphrased to

state that the molecules comprising a gas exert no forces on each other except at impact, travel in straight lines except at instant of collision, are small in size compared to the distance between each other, etc. From these assumptions we can derive the consequences that will occur with changes in pressure, volume, temperature, and so forth, although these were not formally set forth in the assumptions.

3. Theoretical models are formulated with the notion that they are *approximations* of the "true" models largely in terms of the extent to which the holder of a theory must discount other theories as incorrect; the user of a model may recognize that other models of the same phenomena may be useful for purposes other than his own. Put briefly, it is quite possible for two or more models of a system to survive side by side because they serve different purposes adequately. It is not possible for two theories to survive logically side by side unless it can be shown that the differences between them are terminological, i.e., that one theory can be translated directly into the terms of the other. Under these circumstances they are, of course, one theory and not two.

4. A model is often formulated, developed, and even named on the basis of an *analogy* between the object or system described in the model and some different object or system. Thus the billiard-ball model of gases involves an analogy between the properties of a perfectly elastic billiard ball and a molecule in a gas. Now an analogy is never valid in itself unless it can be shown that besides those properties that were formulated in the analogy, others that might be deduced are also empirically confirmed. An analogy then, in this case, is a rough first approximation.

Theories differ from models mainly in that they are more nearly complete and generally more complex. Explanation and systematization by means of a theory are generally regarded as "deeper" or more final than the approximations provided by models. It is possible to use a model while recognizing that it is, in part, incorrect. It may make assumptions that account for some of the empirical data but are discrepant with others. Models may be used when there is, as yet, no comprehensive theory of the data in which the investigator is interested.

For our purposes, we shall use the term "model" in the manner indicated by the description of the four characteristics given above. There are other definitions of the concept of a model, but they may be ignored here as being, for the present, irrelevant to the problems of psychopathology.[1] It will be obvious that the choice of model will determine the kinds of research conducted, measuring procedures used, and significance attributed to data. A clear awareness of the tentativeness of models is absolutely essential for the student of psychopathology, and we shall devote the next chapter to a thorough discussion of current models and their consequences.

RELIABILITY AND VALIDITY

Whatever model the research investigator uses he will be faced with certain technical requirements in regard to the procedures he uses to record and measure events. Many of his problems arise in matters of reliability and validity.

Reliability. A measuring procedure is said to be reliable when repeated applications of it to the same event will produce the same score or number, regardless of who is doing the measuring. One of the more obvious kinds of reliability is *repeat reliability* or *test-retest reliability*. When the measure used is an established psychometric test (intelligence, personality, and the like), it is generally likely that the problem of repeat reliability has been studied during the original construction of the test. This is not always the case, of course, and any competent investigator would ensure this before beginning to use such a test. However, much research in psychopathology involves reponse measures constructed specifically for the experiment in question. The measurement of perceptual constancies, card sorting, object sorting, reaction time, and many other kinds of response measures are equally susceptible to problems of reliability. Where the investigation is one comparing the performance of a normal control group with a pathological group, the repeat reliability of the measure for one group may not be the same as that for the other group. Day-by-day fluctuations in performance are much more common in psychiatric populations than in normal populations. It is very important, therefore, to establish the limits of fluctuation on a particular experimental task if we are to assess the significance of any differences that are found between pathological and normal popula-

[1] Examples of these may be found in Nagel's *The structure of science* (1961) and Braithwaite's *Scientific explanation* (1953). The essence of their views is that a model is a concrete version of an abstract theoretical calculus.

tions. It is equally important to know this if we are to interpret the absence of differences in a valid manner.

Interjudge reliability becomes necessary when an experimenter is using a measure in which some act of judgment is required from an observer. Judgments of the number of aggressive acts in an interpersonal interaction, the number of achievement themes in a story, etc., usually depend upon the use of a preestablished code or category system defining the class of events as precisely as possible. The reliability of the code is to a large extent a function of its lack of ambiguity interacting with a margin of observer error. Reliability may be computed by correlating one observer's scoring of a sequence of behavior with the scores recorded by another observer using the same code.

Validity. Behavioral scientists have generally accepted the terminology of Cronbach and Meehl (1955) in their definitions of validity. Four types of validity were described: *predictive, concurrent, content, and construct.* As an introduction to this problem, we might remark that all kinds of validity have in common the fact that they relate to the accuracy with which a measure correlates with some other kind of observation.

Predictive validity. Predictive validity refers to the empirical accuracy with which the measure can predict some other measure (the criterion) where such a predictive relationship should exist. For example, if the psychopathologist develops a scale that is intended to predict the response of patients to a certain kind of therapy, then the predictive validity of the scale may be established by administering it, providing the therapy, measuring changes occurring in therapy, and correlating this measure with the original scale scores. An illustration of this kind of validity is to be found in the use of the sleep-threshold test reported by Shagass, Naimon, and Mihalik (1956). In this test, the patient is sedated, and the amount of sedative necessary to produce cessation of a simple response is recorded as the sleep-threshold measure. They report that the lower this threshold (the less sedative required to produce cessation), the better the prospects for remission under electroconvulsive shock therapy (ECT).

When the correlation between some measure such as this and a criterion measure is reported, the predictive validity will be influenced by the circumstances under which the correlation was obtained. In the extreme case, we might consider an investigator who is interested in predicting recidivism in the criminal and gives a battery of 20 measures to a group of prisoners. He then waits for their release and subsequent conviction of a new crime, and with these data available computes all 20 correlations with the criterion. One of these correlations proves to be statistically significant (at the .05 level), and he reports this measure as a predictor of recidivism. He had not singled it out as a likely predictor before he computed the correlations, but he simply accepted it after the correlations were known. Under these circumstances, the significance of the correlation might merely reflect the fact that, if one computes 20 correlations from a randomly assorted array of measures, there is considerable prospect that one of them will appear significant at the .05 level. Should this have happened, then when the investigation is replicated it is quite unlikely that the same correlation would again emerge as significant by chance. Hence the true significance of the correlation cannot be assessed until this replication has been done and the same correlation shown to be significant once again. This replication process is known as *cross-validation.*

On the other hand, if the investigator constructs one scale by deducing theoretically what kind of items in a scale should predict recidivism, then the discovery of a significant correlation with the criterion is much more impressive and the question of cross-validity is not crucial.

Concurrent validity. Concurrent validity refers to the accuracy with which one form of a measure may replace another. Typical examples include the use of short time-samples to replace measures usually taken over longer periods of time and the use of short forms of intelligence or personality tests. Although these problems are of some importance in applied clinical research, they are less frequently encountered by the research psychopathologist.

Content validity. Many of the issues of validity which confront the psychopathologist concern the matter of content validity. A measure possesses content validity when it is an appropriate sample of the proposed attribute or construct that it is presumed to measure. Let us consider an investigator who wishes to study differences in dependency between hysterical and normal subjects. He decides to use a task in which the subject is free to turn to the experimenter for help in reaching a solution. A record is made of help-seeking behavior during the experiment, and the two groups are compared on this score. Whether or not the measure has content validity hinges to a large extent on the definition the experimenter had in mind for the concept of dependency. If he meant to refer exclusively to the behavior of seeking help in experimental tasks, then it would be hard to quarrel with his measure, although we might wish to see it replicated with other tasks and other experimenters. On the other hand, if he wished dependency to mean a general tendency to turn to others for help, support, and affection in the face of minor frustration, it is clear that his chosen measure is an extremely limited sample of the broad behavioral pattern concerned.

For the psychopathologist this question is especially likely to arise in connection with the definitional experiment or the experimental analogue (see Chapter 3). If the investigator has noticed that many schizophrenic patients seem to suffer from difficulties in depth perception, he may decide that this observation must be confirmed experimentally. He constructs a depth-perception apparatus consisting of white-painted rods at varying positions in a black box in which the cues to depth may be systematically manipulated. His schizophrenic sample performs as well as the normal control group does, leading him to doubt the validity of the patient's own clinical complaints. However, his experimental task may have carefully eliminated some of the variables that were essential to generating the clinical phenomenon, such as the presence of a meaningful background and surrounding auditory distraction. In other words, it lacked content validity as a sample or representation of the environments that produce the criterion phenomenon.

It is most important to note that this kind of procedure would lack content validity only if the investigator had intended to investigate the validity of the patients' complaints. Had he wished to ascertain whether or not the difficulties experienced by patients extended to perception under conditions of laboratory control, then his procedure would be valid by definition.

Construct validity. Many theoretical notions used by psychopathologists are not directly accessible to observation. Many of them are defined in ways that do not carry with them a potential single measure of the underlying process to which the construct refers. Anxiety, for example, is commonly used to refer to a pattern of behaviors that includes verbal expressions of fear, changes in autonomic system functioning, and overt avoidance responses in the presence of certain classes of situations. None of these three classes of response correlates perfectly with either of the other two. Some individuals will express fear or show autonomic arousal or do both but will not run away from a threatening stimulus. Other combinations are found frequently. Clearly there is no "true" measure of anxiety against which we can assess the validity of the other measures. Now when an investigator wishes to develop an additional measure of anxiety, he will tend to examine its validity with reference to all these measures, accepting good correlations with all of them as satisfactory but not necessarily expecting perfect correlations with any one of them. If the construct "anxiety" has further theoretical implications—such as those bearing on the conditionability of anxious people—then the investigator will seek additional validation of the new measure through studies of its ability to predict conditionability in the correct direction. Groups of measures connected with each other through a network of correlations and developed from a common core construct thus provide mutual validity where no one measure is the final criterion.

Psychopathologists are vitally concerned with construct validity when they are testing a hypothesis that rests upon the general validity of a construct and its defining measures. Thus, in studying the hypothesis that psychopathic patients are less anxious than psychoneurotic patients, it is necessary to use a measure, or measures, of anxiety that have already been shown to have construct validity in a reasonably wide range of other situations. Many etiological hypotheses involve a research strategy that depends upon the construct validity of some of the measures to be used. We might consider the hypothesis that schizophrenia is a disorder of attention in which the prime deficit lies in an inability to inhibit distracting stimuli. Attention is a construct, an inference from the correlations among various kinds of responses. One measure of attention is the lack of disruption of performance in a task under distracting conditions. Another measure is the efficiency of recall of a series of stimuli presented for only a limited time. Another is the lack of perception of peripheral stimuli when the subject is instructed to respond specifically to central stimuli. As research data accumulate indicating that schizophrenic patients do show impairment under all these conditions and that this is coupled with frequent spontaneous verbal complaints of difficulty in "concentrating," we are seeing the simultaneous establishment of construct validity for various measures of attention and the accumulation of support for the etiological hypothesis.

When an etiological hypothesis has gained much support from studies using different measures, then the failure of a new measuring technique to produce supportive evidence may be a reflection upon the construct validity of the new technique rather than upon the validity of the etiological hypothesis.

Discriminant validity. Although not included in the four kinds of validity identified by Cronbach and Meehl (1955), it is important to give some attention to what has been called discriminant validity (cf. Campbell & Fiske, 1959). Several measures of a construct may correlate because they are related to a process other than that envisaged by the theory in which the construct is embedded. We might imagine a situation in which all the measures of attention deficit were confounded with some difficulty of a physical kind involving auditory perception: the subjects perform poorly on the task because they cannot hear the instructions clearly. Thus, while the measures used might be validly reactive to deficiencies of attention, they are also excessively reactive to other phenomena. All measures, even in the more precise realms of the physical sciences, tend to react to undesired sources of variance; for example, the springs in a weighing balance will be slightly affected by changes in temperature. Complete freedom from influence by anything except the parameter of interest is an impractical ideal, especially in the current state of the behavioral sciences. However, it is possible to establish the extent to which the correlation of the measure with the desired criterion exceeds its correlations with irrelevant factors. If the two correlations are equal or if the correlation with the desired criterion (however high in absolute figures) is less than that with irrelevant factors, then the measure does not have adequate discriminant validity and requires modification.

Ordinarily an investigator will also seek to control the effect of irrelevant variance by selecting his subjects and experimental situation in such a fashion as to exclude it. Thus he will administer his measures of attention with suitable precautions to ensure that the subjects understand the instructions, using a trial period or other preliminary check. However, when the hypothesis to be tested is that one of the groups will show a *deficit* in performance, some more careful check on the discriminant validity of the measures may be necessary.

Sensitivity. Measures must have more than reliability and the appropriate kind of validity. They must also possess adequate sensitivity.

Sensitivity refers to the power of the measure to detect and distinguish among small differences in the value of the parameter measured. A weighing machine that issued printed tickets recording weight to the nearest 5 pounds would be considerably less sensitive than one built to print out results to the nearest ounce, although both might involve valid application of the principles of weight measurement. Behavioral measures may be insensitive for many reasons. Seeking to find differences in learning ability between a normal and pathological group, the experimenter may select a learning task that is too easy—everyone learns it rapidly—or too difficult—nobody learns it in the time allotted. Thus, no differences will be found although fundamental differences between the groups might exist.

SAMPLING AND CONTROLS

Armed with an appropriate hypothesis and with measures suitable to test it, the research investigator must next turn to consider other sources of error that might damage his work. Many of these may be discussed as aspects of the techniques of sampling and control.

Sampling. When an investigator selects a sample of subjects for his research, he is guided by two main considerations. The first is the nature of the population to which he wishes to generalize his results; the second is the extent to which irrelevant, but confounding, sources of error are likely to exist in his sample. If he wishes to make some general comparison between, let us say, the life expectancy of senile patients and that of normal patients of the same age, then his main concern is that his selection of samples from both populations has no inadvertent bias. Patients in public hospitals may have a poorer socioeconomic history and thus a poorer nutritional history than patients in private nursing homes. The investigator will want to ensure that his sample comes from both kinds of hospitals and that other possible distortions are also eliminated at the outset. Once he has arranged matters so that any member of the population *might* be selected, then he may use a random method for the actual selection. With a suitable size, his sample should be proportionately representative of the characteristics of the total population.

His normal group is selected in like manner—it being necessary to ensure that each member of the total normal population, or some very large segment of it, stands an equal chance of being selected. If the purpose of the investigation is to ascertain simply whether or not there is a difference and no theoretical explanation is at stake, then this method of sampling will be adequate. When the difference has been established, the natural consequence will be the development of hypotheses to account for it. An obvious preliminary step is to look for other significant differences between the two samples. When these are found, they may form the basis of an explanatory hypothesis—they do not provide evidence for the validity of such a hypothesis. For example, let us assume that a difference is found in the socioeconomic status of two groups and that the original sampling has ensured that this is not due to bias in the method of sample selection. We may wish to test the hypothesis that the difference in life expectancy is related to the socioeconomic-status variable and not to the presence of senility. Now it becomes necessary to select samples that differ in socioeconomic status but are equally senile. Our sampling has *controlled* for senility while varying socioeconomic status. Should senility now turn out to be irrelevant, then we may accept the socioeconomic hypothesis and develop a new hypothesis to account for that difference. Now we may suggest that nutritional differences are the important variable, in which case we will want to draw samples from low socioeconomic-status populations but with differing, i.e., good versus bad, nutritional histories.

Although the foregoing series of steps is a simplified but logical description of the manner in which sampling controls may be used, few modern investigations are conducted in such a naïve manner. The hypothetical experimenter will probably try to test all the plausible hypotheses at the same time by drawing samples that represent different values of each parameter, i.e., several levels of socioeconomic status, several levels of senility for each level of socioeconomic status, and several levels of nutritional history for each of these combinations. However, he will permit differences only in those factors that he wishes to test; his samples will otherwise be the same on all other variables.

If an investigator knew exactly what factors might influence his results beyond the experimental or manipulated factor, there would be no need for large samples. We might imagine (in a moment of fantasy) that we knew with complete certainty that the only normal factor affecting reaction time was chronological age. Wishing to test the hypothesis that brain injury may produce pathological deficiencies in reaction time, we should be able to test the hypothesis, in principle, by using only one brain-injured subject matched for age with one normal subject. However, we cannot know that only one or some limited number of factors might influence behavior in an experiment, and hence, we must use large samples on the assumption that all normal values of the unknown influences will be distributed similarly in both groups. Furthermore, on many kinds of psychopathological dimensions there is considerable risk that some of the normal controls will overlap with the experimental group. A small proportion of subjects who would be classified as non-schizophrenic (i.e., never diagnosed as schizophrenic) will, in fact, be behaviorally schizoid. On various measures of schizophrenicity they may overlap with the experimental group of diagnosed schizophrenics. In order to reduce the effect that this kind of subject will have on the results, it is necessary also to draw reasonably large samples. Unfortunately, large samples are generally difficult to obtain with any degree of assurance that they are homogeneous in diagnosis.

Control of variables. Once the samples have been selected, the design of a study may be described in terms of *independent* and *dependent* variables. The independent variable is what is presumed to influence the value taken by the dependent variable. By way of a rough approximation, we might say that stimuli used in studies are generally the independent variables, and the responses they elicit are the dependent variables. In a genuine experiment all independent variables are under the investigator's control. Within the setting of the experiment they are allowed to vary only in some systematic fashion and in measured amounts. Since it is not practicable to manipulate directly the independent variable of the psychopathological status of a subject, this is achieved by the processes of selection described in the previous paragraphs. Thus the selection of neurotic versus normal groups serves to introduce neurosis-normalcy as an independent variable. Some methodologists would deny that this kind of selection produces an independent variable in the strict sense of the term. This matter is given further discussion in our description of the correlational experiment in Chapter 3. In the duodenal ulcer experiment, the army stress was a true independent variable (although only crudely controlled), and gastric secretion is essentially a partially independent variable.

We may distinguish between the *direct* and *remote* control of the independent variable. For example, we may wish to study the effect of a stress such as noise upon complex skilled behavior. Direct control of the independent variable, noise, is readily available with appropriate apparatus. On the other hand, we may wish to study the effects of high arousal upon the performance of the task and may have selected noise as a suitable way of inducing arousal. Provided that we have an agreed-upon criterion of measure of arousal—such as an increase in heart rate —then we may monitor the effects of noise to make sure that it is producing the intended change in arousal. On the other hand, there may be no universally valid criterion for the intervening state. When this is the case, the assumption that the independent variable is the intervening state is, in fact, an assumption. A failure to find a predicted effect may well occur because the manipulated variable did not succeed in producing the intended state in the subject. Thus, whether or not the independent variable has been adequately manipulated in an experiment is a function of the investigator's intention—not of the kind of physical stimulation he has used.

This brief résumé of the major elements of control will provide the necessary vocabulary for understanding much psychopathological research. It will also serve as a preparation for the more detailed consideration of theoretical models in psychopathology to which we shall now turn.

Summary

In this chapter we have considered the definition of psychopathology and the gross distinctions between *neurosis* and *psychosis*. Loss of reality contact has been suggested as the central basis for this distinction. We have also examined the characteristics of *hypotheses, laws, theories,* and *models* together with an account of the various sources from which hypotheses might arise. Problems of *reliability* and *validity* of measures have been examined: basic principles of *sampling* and the *control* of variables have been introduced. This particular group of concepts and terms provides the basic language for the analysis of detailed research problems in the subsequent chapters.

CHAPTER 2

MODELS FOR THE STUDY OF PSYCHOPATHOLOGY

We shall now consider the major theoretical models used to guide research in psychopathology. As we have seen, a model is a tentative formulation and one that frequently involves an analogy to some other process or scientific explanation for the presentation of its own elements. We have also noted that a model is neither "correct" nor "incorrect" in a formal sense; it may be simply more or less *useful*. Evaluation of a model consists, therefore, mainly in an assessment of the advantages it presents weighed against the distortions and ambiguities it may create. Such evaluations are of value in comparing one model with another plausible alternative. Particular disadvantages may not necessarily lead us to discard a model until a better alternative has been developed.

The Medical Model

By far the most common model in current use is derived from medicine. In general, the medical model rests upon the assumption that the person showing disordered behavior is *sick,* that he is suffering from something called a *disease,* and that, while the disease has some kind of quasi-existence within the *patient,* it may be evident to the observer mainly through a group of more or less obvious *symptoms.* The disease generally has a more or less specific cause or *etiology,* and in many, although not all, diseases the appropriate treatment involves eliminating or controlling the etiological agent. In order to do this, it is essential that the physician identify the etiology correctly, for many different diseases have some symptoms in common. Identifying the etiology is termed *diagnosis* and is usually a prerequisite for deciding upon the appropriate *therapy.*

Diagnosis is usually confirmed by the application of special measurement methods in the laboratory, such as x-ray or blood analysis, which have the power to detect information not available to more superficial inspection. When the diagnosis cannot be confirmed in this way, simply watching the development of the *course* of the disease may make the diagnosis clearer. Provided that a diagnosis is possible and that there is sufficient knowledge about the course of the disease, it becomes possible to make a *prognosis* or forecast of the probable outcome for the patient.

For the psychopathologist, a problematic feature of the medical model is the distinction between the symptoms of a disease and the fundamental disease process itself. When we say that recurring fever is a symptom of tuberculosis, we mean that this is a visible but secondary consequence of a process going on inside the patient of which the essential element is the presence and activity of a specific bacillus. Treating the fever by applying ice packs, giving alcohol rubs, and so forth, may reduce the fever, i.e., remove the symptom, but these treatments have no effect upon the bacillus. Hence it is both possible and necessary to draw a distinction between *symptomatic treatment* and other, more radical forms of therapy. Symptomatic treatment is ordinarily only temporary or palliative, and, should the treatment be discontinued, the symptoms will reappear.

Although these are the features of the medical model that have theoretical interest for us, there are some additional, semantic consequences that have other practical effects. Knowledge of disease processes is a complex and difficult skill to acquire. When a patient falls ill with some disease, it is sometimes impossible for the physician to explain in technical detail what the problem is; if he could, it would not always be possible for every patient to understand him. Consequently, the relationship between physician and patient is one in which the latter obeys "doctor's orders" without always understanding why they are necessary. In short, the patient is obedient to and dependent upon the physician. This is not intrinsic to the disease concept but is partly a result of the complexity of medical science and partly a residue of the religious-magical tradition in the relationship between the healer and the healed. It is found, of course, in many situations in which a layman is dealing with a technical expert.

An additional consequence of the use of medical terminology is the effect that this has upon public attitudes toward the patient. When a patient overeats to the point of obesity, he may provoke attitudes of rejection from his associates for his apparent inability to control this self-indulgence. Should it turn out that the patient is suffering from a glandular disorder of which overeating is a symptom, then he is reclassified as "sick"; rejection may then give place to sympathy and support. Thus, the medical model brings with it not only the use of science to diagnose and treat the patient but also the tolerance of the patient's symptoms by the public.

This account of the medical model is necessarily somewhat oversimplified. Many kinds of problems that do not fit this structure neatly come into the physician's hands. He may have little or no idea about the etiology of the disorder of which the patient complains. Nevertheless he may be able to treat it "empirically," i.e., with a therapy found effective with similar cases in the past, although the manner in which the therapy works may be quite unclear. For example, ECT is used in the treatment of depression because it often seems to have a favorable effect. At present an adequate theoretical explanation of this effect is lacking. For the physician the medical model is not a "model" at all. It is, of course, a set of concepts and terms that physicians have found useful in thinking about their problems and in organizing their research and therapeutic efforts. When these terms and concepts are applied to disordered behavior, they comprise a model. Accordingly, the ultimate validity of the model depends upon the extent to which medical concepts are valid in accounting for the data of psychopathology. In recent decades, there has been a growing awareness of the logical and empirical deficiencies of the medical model, and attempts have been made to develop more workable alternatives for the study of disordered behavior. It will be helpful to consider here the nature of these criticisms and the potential utility of some of the suggested alternatives.

CRITICISM OF THE MEDICAL MODEL

Limitations of diagnosis. The first significant criticism of the medical model in psychopathology revolves around the concept of diagnosis. Diagnoses may take three forms, *etiological, descriptive,* and *prognostic.* An etiological diagnosis is made when the diagnostician examines the available evidence and concludes that further search will show the presence of a specific etiological agent. This kind of diagnosis is possible only when research has previously established the causative relationship between this agent (sometimes called the *pathogen*) and the external symptoms. At the present time behavior disorders are so little understood that the number of etiological diagnoses that can be made with confidence are very few. Paresis, occurring as a consequence of syphilis, is the classic example of a situation in which a particular pattern of behavioral symptoms will permit an etiological diagnosis. Certain other special kinds of toxic psychosis may also be diagnosed etiologically, and the same is true of some disordered behavior that follows from brain injury.

However, the overwhelming majority of psychopathological diagnoses are *descriptive*. A descriptive diagnosis is made when the clinician observes the set of symptoms presented by a patient and then decides which of several possible classifying labels should be applied to his behavior. The label, however, adds no information and implies no additional predictions about what might be found on laboratory examination or what the prognosis will be. Faced with a patient who is hallucinating and has shown some minor signs of loss of interest in his personal appearance, the clinician may spend some considerable time pondering the decision of whether to apply the label "paranoid schizophrenia" or "hebephrenic schizophrenia." Given the facts that we neither know what the significant determinants of schizophrenia are nor have any adequate therapy, the diagnostic procedure serves mainly a statistical and record-keeping purpose. In this sense, the diagnostic process is not closely analogous to that existing in physical medicine, and the very use of the term "diagnosis" to describe it gives the misleading impression that something informative is being done in the same way that it is done in a medical diagnosis.

Now while the criticisms leveled at descriptive diagnosis are valid enough when considered in the light of current psychiatric diagnostic practices, it should be emphasized that the concept of etiological diagnosis is perfectly sound; we should not slip into the position of deciding, as some psychologists have, that any kind of diagnosis is intrinsically inappropriate. Diagnosis that identifies the determinants of a set of consequences, whether in psychopathology or in a defective radio, is an essential part of both the development of science and the discovery of appropriate remedies.

Even though we have seen that descriptive diagnosis may be criticized as misleading when it is allowed to substitute for etiological diagnosis, we should note that it serves an important purpose in the early study of natural phenomena. Before we can begin to search effectively for the origins of a specific pattern of events, we must have established a reasonably good definition of the pattern and have been assured that it tends to recur with some internal regularity. The position has been well put by Eysenck (1960) as follows: "Before we can reasonably be asked to look for the cause of a particular dysfunction or disorder, we must have isolated, however crudely, the dysfunction or disorder in question, and we must be able to recognize it and differentiate it from other syndromes [p. 1]."

In this sense descriptive "diagnosis," i.e., classification, is the prerequisite for a systematic search for determinants; it is the starting point for research, not the terminal point in describing a patient.

Stability and reliability of diagnosis. For the psychopathologist, the problems generated by the current system of diagnostic classification are largely the consequence of the manner in which the system developed. In observing the behavior of a patient, there are many events that might be used to establish a classification system—just as in developing filing systems for a bookshelf. The first step, before any decision about the basis for classification is made, is to establish empirically patterns of events that tend to occur together reliably. Historically, these regularities were observed by individual clinicians using nonquantitative methods. Consequently, the decision that some group of symptoms constituted a reliable pattern (a *syndrome*) rested on the accuracy, objectivity, and breadth of experience of individual clinicians. As we shall see later, observers are liable to err in many ways, not the least of which is the tendency to record what is both obvious and dramatic to the neglect of seemingly lesser items.

With recent advances in computer technology and methods of statistical inference, as well as in the development of new devices for recording behavior (the cinema camera, tape recorder, telemetry, etc.), it has become possible to study behavior syndromes with much greater sophistication than in the past. Under the circumstances, therefore, it is not surprising to find that syndromes discovered in this way do not correspond exactly to those derived from loose clinical observation. In Table 2-1 we may compare the four classic syndromes of schizophrenia with a set of schizophrenic "types" produced by statistical analysis of the behavior of many schizophrenic patients.

Inspection of this table shows that there are some groupings that appear to be reliably produced both by clinical observation and statistical methods (notably the paranoid and catatonic categories) but that others show very little correspondence between the two systems. Whether the statistical system is more valid than the clinical-descriptive method will depend in the long run on whether or not the types turn out to have reliably different, discoverable etiologies.

Quite apart from the possible weaknesses of clinical observation in arriving at plausible categories is the fundamental problem of the reliability of the diagnostic description. The situation might be likened to the hypothesis that a man's character can be estimated from the

Table 2.1   Classifications of Schizophrenia Derived from Statistical Methods Compared with Those Derived from Clinical Observation

Statistical methods [1]	*Clinical observation* [2]
CATATONIC-WITHDRAWN Mannerisms or gestures Some positioning Slowed movements Place disorientation	**CATATONIC** Stupor and excitement Motor symptoms, immobility, etc. Negativism Onset often acute
OVEREXPRESSIVE Assertive Generally hostile Generally initiates conversation Overtalkative	**HEBEPHRENIC** Silliness, incongruous behavior Fragmentary delusions Some hallucinations Neologisms, mannerisms Asocial appearance, grooming
PARANOID Bizarre thoughts Generally hostile Influenced by persecutors Can show hostility to personnel	**PARANOID** Delusions predominate Hallucinations (usually auditory) Suspiciousness, aloofness
RESISTIVE-ISOLATION May dislike being told what to do Underactive Social avoidance Not dependable	**SIMPLE** Gradual loss of interest, slow onset No emotional outbursts Absence of hallucinations Declining social adequacy
ANXIOUS-DYSPHORIC Expresses despondency Recognizes illness Overconcerned about others' opinion Some fear of doom	

Sources: [1] Guertin, W. H. Empirical syndrome groupings of schizophrenic hospital admissions. *Journal of Clinical Psychology*, 1961, **17**, 268–275.

[2] Cameron, N. The functional psychoses. In J. McV. Hunt (Ed.), *Personality and the behavior disorders.* New York: Ronald Press, 1944.

strength of his handshake. Before we can begin to examine the plausibility of the hypothesis, we must be sure that strength of handshake can be measured with some reliability. By the same token, before we can decide whether or not the category of paranoid schizophrenia is a meaningful one, we must be sure that two or more observers can apply the category to the same patient and come up with the same label. This is the problem of interjudge reliability discussed in Chapter 1. Until this kind of reliability has been established for a system of classification, it is not possible to investigate the validity of the classifications in any sensible manner. Psychiatric classification has been subject to much scrutiny with regard to interjudge reliability; unfortunately the results are somewhat ambiguous. Studies conducted up to 1955 (e.g., Ash, 1949; Raines & Rohrer, 1955) reported discouraging results, the chief tenor of which was that the diagnosis depended as much upon the psychiatrist who made it as it did upon the patient who was presented to be diagnosed by him. Agreements among psychiatrists ranged from a low level of 34 percent on very specific diagnostic categories, such as "schizoid type" versus "paranoid type" of conduct disorder, to 67 percent in diagnosing broad categories such as "psychosis" versus "conduct disorder" (Ash, 1949).

However, these early studies have been criticized by Beck (1962). He has pointed out that they have been marred by various methodological flaws of which the major ones are these:

1. Unequal amounts of information about each patient available for diagnosing
2. Differences in the amount of training and experience of the psychiatrists making the diagnostic judgments
3. Long time intervals between the judgments, permitting the possibility that the behavior of the patient had changed
4. The use of items other than the orthodox psychiatric criteria to make the diagnosis

In some subsequent studies these variables have been controlled, and higher degrees of agreement have been reported. For example, Sandifer, Pettus, and Quade (1964) report 74 percent agreement for schizophrenia and 56 percent for diagnoses of neurosis. In summarizing these and other studies of reliability, Buss (1966) concludes:

Psychoses, taken generically, can be diagnosed with considerable reliability. There is some evidence that one psychosis, schizophrenia, can be diagnosed reliably. Thus, the commonly held belief in the unreliability of psychiatric diagnoses is incorrect or at best only partly correct. Specific diagnoses and diagnoses of the milder forms of psychopathology tend to be unreliable [p. 41].

The problem still remains somewhat unresolved, however, since none of the studies cited indicate the extent to which agreement on diagnostic categories might be arrived at by chance, given the base rate for the specific diagnosis. For example, if one clinician diagnoses schizophrenia in 80 percent of all patients that he sees and the same percentage is found in the diagnoses of the second psychiatrist, then they will agree by chance 64 percent of the time. On the other hand, if they apply the diagnosis of conduct disorder only 10 percent of the time, then their chance agreement will be only 1 percent. Without knowledge of the base rates of the two judges, it is not possible to decide by simple inspection whether a particular percentage of agreement is satisfactory or not. In the hypothetical instances cited above, 70 percent agreement in the category of schizophrenia would be less impressive than 30 percent agreement in the category of conduct disorder. The most appropriate method of resolving this kind of disagreement would involve presenting a clinician with equal proportions of the various diagnostic categories as diagnosed by another clinician so that the matter of unequal probabilities of the different diagnostic categories could be controlled adequately.

Validity of Diagnosis. Whether or not a typical clinician can make reliable diagnoses is, in the long run, less important than the validity or utility of the category itself. Thus, although reliability is an essential prerequisite for validity, it is the validity which is of ultimate importance to science. In its most optimistic form, the issue of diagnostic usefulness has been put by Kraepelin in the following way:

Judging from our experience in internal medicine, it is a fair assumption that similar disease processes will produce identical symptom pictures, identical pathological anatomy, and an identical etiology. If, therefore, we possessed a comprehensive knowledge of any one of these three fields—pathological anatomy, symptomatology, or etiology—we would at once have a uniform and standard classification of mental diseases. A similar comprehensive knowledge of either of the other two fields would give not only just as uniform and standard classifications but all these classifications would exactly coincide. Cases of mental disorder originating in the same cause must also present the same symptoms and the same pathological findings [Kraepelin, quoted by Diefendorf, 1921, p. 200].

Etiological validity. From this point of view, the validity of a diagnosis may be established by showing empirically that there is a significant difference between subjects with one diagnosis and subjects with other diagnoses in terms either of what may be discovered about their early history or of their response to particular kinds of treatment. By "early history" here is meant the record not only of environmental experiences but also of biological events, trauma, infections, genetic endowment, and so on. If a diagnostic system of categories does not have a significant relationship to either of these two criteria—etiology and therapy—then it is functionally invalid.

At this point the psychopathologist runs the risk of becoming entangled in a circular net of ambiguities. It is quite possible to develop hypotheses about the probable etiology of a diagnostic category, to seek empirical evidence that the hypothesis is correct, and to fail to find it. When this happens, it may be because the hypothesis is incorrect (there really is a uniform etiology for the syndrome, but it is not the one that was hypothesized); it may be because the method used in the research was inadequate to test the hypothesis for any one of a number of technical reasons; or it may be because the syndrome has no etiological unity, and thus the search for a specific etiology is a wild goose chase.

For the psychopathologist, the problem is to judge in each case the probable source of the negative findings. Obviously there is no single point at which it may be decided that the diagnostic category is invalid, in the sense that there is definite "proof" of its invalidity. Instead, there tends to be a growing disillusionment with a category system when repeated tests of many different kinds of etiological hypotheses have failed to produce significant findings. From a practical point of view, even this disillusionment may not bring about any perceptible abandonment of the category system; this happens only when an alternative system with some demonstrable validity has been found to replace it. Since this validity cannot be found without much research, it becomes a characteristic of research in psychopathology (as distinguished from clinical usage) that the investigator often concerns himself with categories that are tentative and do not accord with contemporary clinical usage.

Because of this state of affairs, it is not presently possible to state that the current system of psychiatric nosology is or is not valid. All that can be done is to point to the conclusions drawn from surveys of the massive quantities of research data that have been accumulated over the past several decades. Cameron (1944) commented: "All current attempts at classification of functional personality disorders are unsatisfactory; this is true for the neuroses as well as the psychoses [p. 870]." Twenty-two years later, Buss (1966) concluded that "present classifications offer little information on etiology; schizophrenia, for example, appears to have many different causes [p. 42]." However, the urgency of the problem has now been recognized more widely, and we may be fairly confident that another two decades will not lead us to a similarly uninspiring conclusion.

Levels of etiology. Before leaving the issue of diagnosis, we should note that the concept of etiology is itself a rather ambiguous one. When a pathological outcome occurs, the sequence of determinants preceding it may be quite complex and may stretch over some period of time. Let us examine the hypothetical instance of a man who comes to the hospital with complaints that he has fallen on an icy driveway, banging his head on the ground, and now has a headache and feels dizzy. He attributes his fall to carelessness due to preoccupation with business worries. The physician may decide that the probable diagnosis is that the skull is fractured and may seek to confirm this via x-ray examination. It may seem to be belaboring the obvious to point out that there are several possible levels at which the etiology of these symptoms might be defined. A violent blow to the head is the etiology of the fracture in the most direct sense: slipping on ice was the etiology of the violent blow: preoccupation with matters other than the ground underfoot was the etiology of the fall on the ice. Now as we examine this pyramid of etiologies, we notice that the further we get from the moment of the direct etiology, the less specific the etiology becomes for the fracturing of a skull. Thus, while the overwhelming majority of skull fractures have etiologies that involve violent impact upon the skull itself, many fewer have etiologies that involve preoccupation with business worries. As an event becomes less certain to produce a specific pathology, there is an increasing likelihood that it may produce various other pathologies. Thus, a fall on the ice may lead to a fractured hip, arm, or leg, or merely to bruises.

Further consideration of this reveals that knowledge of the direct etiology of a pathological condition may be crucial in deciding an appropriate therapy, whereas knowledge of the indirect etiologies may be quite irrelevant. Patients with broken skulls are treated along certain lines regardless of whether the fracture occurred after a fall on the ice or in a football game. Knowledge of the indirect etiologies may be of value, however, in planning programs of prevention. Keeping icy roads clear reduces accidental fractures of all kinds and thus would be important in a program of accident prevention.

Research in psychopathology, where the problem is that of the etiological validity of a diagnostic category, may be hampered unless the researcher is quite clear about the level of etiology to which his hypothesis refers. If it is relatively indirect, then the finding that only a few of his subjects have histories of the kind he expected need not compel the conclusion that his hypothesis is fundamentally incorrect but may compel the conclusion that it is dealing with an etiological factor some distance removed from the pathological event.

Prognostic validity. Although the unsatisfactory nature of our present understanding of the etiologies of psychopathology is generally acknowledged, the validity of current classification schemes for *prognosis* is more controversial.

Meehl (1959) has claimed that the prognostic homogeneity among patients belonging to a given diagnostic group is sufficient that "assignment of a patient to this group has probability implications which it is clinically unsound to ignore [p. 103]." Certainly there are well-established statistical regularities in the probability of discharge from the hospital for patients in different diagnostic categories, and statements that a patient has a "good" or "poor" prognosis may be made with confidence that exceeds chance levels. Perhaps it would be fairest to state that the problem is not the utter invalidity of the current system of classification for prognostic purposes but rather the urgency of improving it to levels of validity more in keeping with the seriousness of the problem of psychopathology.

In the space available, it is not possible to summarize what is known about the prognostic validities of specific diagnostic groups, but reviews abound in the scientific literature (e.g., Ash, 1949; Hoch & Zubin, 1953; Mehlman, 1952; Zigler & Phillips, 1961), and the reader of this book will undoubtedly turn to them.

THE MEDICAL MODEL: CRITICAL MISUNDERSTANDINGS

The failure to find adequate validities, etiological or prognostic, for current classification schemes has led some psychopathologists to conclude that the problem is inherent in classification itself. Thus, the medical analogy is rejected not only because the concept of unitary syndromes has borne a disappointingly small practical yield but also because medical analogies are thought inevitably to carry with them the necessity of thinking in terms of separate disease entities. Such a criticism is, in fact, an underestimate of the sophistication of physicians' thinking about diseases. For certain classes of bodily pathology, the entity classification has been very useful and is employed in medicine without much qualm. Thus, the infectious diseases, in which etiology resides in a pathogenic organism, have been treated very effectively upon the assumption that the appropriate therapy would involve selective destruction of the pathogen by chemical means, i.e., the antibiotics. This approach has meant the classification of pathogens, the identification of syndromes, and so forth. In fact, it would be only a mild exaggeration to remark that what many behavioral scientists mean by the medical model is really the "infectious-disease model."

Medical practitioners have not found it necessary to adopt only one kind of disease model in thinking about bodily disorders; they adopt instead a range of models to suit their practical uses. Many disease terms are not entity terms at all. Cancer is a concept that applies quite loosely to a range of pathological conditions with many probable etiologies. Traumatic mechanical injuries to tissues can be dealt with without previous efforts to decide upon an appropriate entity categorization for every conceivable injury. Physicians have generally recognized the continuity of bodily influences upon many systematic diseases such as hypertension and arthritis. The reader should understand, therefore, that most criticisms of the "medical" model deal with only one kind of model used in the medical sciences and are irrelevant to much of the conceptual development that has occurred with noninfectious diseases.

The Dynamic Model

While much research has been conducted by psychopathologists looking for etiologies of the classic syndromes, another considerable effort has consisted of attempts to demonstrate the validity of existing psychoanalytic hypotheses about the etiology of these disorders. In the space available to us here, we may examine the major tenets of the theory insofar as they produce hypotheses of interest to psychopathology, and also look at matters of methodology germane to testing these hypotheses. A thorough analysis of psychoanalytic theory would be beyond the scope of this work, but excellent presentations are available elsewhere.[1]

Psychoanalytic theory is structured upon certain formal assumptions. A prime assumption is that human behavior may be represented as the outcome of an energy system. One of Freud's definitions of the theory was that it was "a dynamic conception which reduces mental life to an interplay of reciprocally urging and checking forces [Healy, Bronner, & Bowers, 1930, p. xv]." This energy stems mainly from, or is defined by, the sexual instincts. However, these sexual instincts are broadly defined, consisting in their nucleus of physical sexuality but also including self-love, friendship, family love, love of humanity, love of things, and love of abstract ideas. For Freud it seemed established that these latter were all expressions of the fundamental sexual instinct. To this energy psychoanalysis gave the name *libido*. This is characterized by certain attributes. It may vary in intensity even in the same individual; it is always present even in early childhood, though differing from normal manifestations; it is not confined to the sexual organs alone but becomes attached in succession to a variety of bodily areas related to nutrition and excretion and, finally, procreation.

Although the succession of "attachments" is predetermined, the effects of various environmental influences during the attachment will de-

[1] The reader is referred particularly to Hendrick, *Facts and theories of psychoanalysis.* New York: Knopf, 1958, and to the earlier standard work of Healy, Bronner, & Bowers, *The structure and meaning of psychoanalysis.* New York: Knopf, 1930.

termine the character of the individual on a more or less permanent basis. This process is called *fixation* and represents one of the ways in which the distribution of libidinal energy may be channeled. This and other consequences have been summarized thus:

> The distribution of libido, that is, the direction of the libidinal flow, is constantly changing. It may, for example, be directed inward or outward (object love and narcism), it may be arrested in its forward flow (fixation), or it may flow to levels representing earlier stages of development (regression), it may become dammed up (repression), or it may be deflected into other more socially acceptable channels (sublimation) [Healy et al., 1930, p. 6].

As we examine this set of propositions, it appears at first sight that the psychoanalyst is using an energy model in which the motivation of human behavior is seen as being "like" a source of physical energy and is more specifically likened to hydrodynamic energy (waterpower) "flowing" through a sequence of "channels" and being "dammed" or "deflected" at various "levels." However, a more careful scrutiny reveals that what is being described here is not a model but a metaphor. None of the operations that a physicist uses to measure "flow" or "direction" or to define "level" or "dam" are being employed by the psychoanalyst. We have seen that when a gas physicist uses the billiard-ball model of the molecular action of gases, he uses the terms "impact," "straight line," and "size" in exactly the same way—using the same measuring operations—to compare the activity of both billiard balls and molecules. In the case of psychoanalysis, the measuring procedures used to define the damming up of hydrodynamic energy bear no relation to the theoretical constructs noted. Hence the energy concept in psychoanalysis does not represent the temporary borrowing of an existing and useful concept from another science but simply represents the selection of terms with picturesque connotations.

This fact in itself would not represent a weakness in the theoretical position of psychoanalysis, provided that new sets of operations were established to define the borrowed terms. The difficulties surrounding research in psychoanalytic theory are mainly attributable to a failure to provide such operational definitions.

Although psychoanalytic theory makes much use of the energy metaphor, the application of the theory to psychopathology has tended to be constrained by the classic system of disease categories in psychiatry.

Thus Freud did not find it necessary or possible to consider what new categories of disorder might stem from his theoretical assumptions but rather accepted the existing categories such as paranoid schizophrenia and hysteria. He defined the task of the psychoanalytically oriented psychopathologist as the discovery of the specific pattern of energy disturbance that provides the etiology for an already identified syndrome. Thus, repression of sexuality was of major importance in the genesis of hysteria, denial of homosexuality in the formation of paranoid ideation, etc.

Since repression, fixation, and the other disturbances of energy flow are assumed to result from environmental experiences, and since the energy phenomena are not measureable directly (or even defined in potentially measurable fashion), then the final empirical links to which research might be directed are reduced in principle to two. One line of research seeks to demonstrate that certain kinds of childhood experience lead to later psychopathology; thus, for example, efforts have been made to test the hypothesis that severe toilet-training techniques produce obsessive-compulsive syndromes. A second kind of research seeks to demonstrate that the individual showing some standard symptoms of psychopathology also shows hitherto undetected symptoms when special measurement techniques are applied; for example, the development of tests to demonstrate that the paranoid schizophrenic will tend to see homosexuality in the behavior of others more than a control subject would.

Research strategies of this kind are very valuable and are used by psychopathologists of many different theoretical persuasions. In fact, the superfluity of the energy concept should not blind the reader to the possible utility of testing psychoanalytic hypotheses at the empirical level, regardless of the metaphorical nature of the theoretical superstructure. For the psychopathologist, however, psychoanalytic hypotheses, as they are generally formulated, have many implicit methodological difficulties. Let us look at some of them here.

CRITICISMS OF THE PSYCHOANALYTIC MODEL

Lack of observer agreement. Psychoanalysts frequently allege that the method of controlled experimentation is inherently inappropriate to the testing of their hypotheses. The privacy of the consulting room and the relationship of patient to therapist is considered a *sine qua non* for the demonstration of the theory's validity. For many years this argument has been relatively successful in defending against the unfavorable results obtained from controlled experiments because it precluded the use of multiple observers and made it impossible to apply the criterion of observer agreement to the analyst's observations. With the greater availability of the cinema camera, closed-circuit television, and the tape recorder, the argument is vitiated, and it may be that we shall soon see attempts to acquire the necessary evidence.

Confusion of inference and observation.   An observation consists of the recording of events occurring in the physical realm. These may be movements, spoken sounds, written marks, movements of a needle on a measuring gauge, etc. Observations are primary in the sense that they are the point from which theorizing starts. Data gathered by observation are used to make inferences which may or may not be correct. Thus, examining the pen markings on a cardiogram may lead a cardiologist to infer something about the state of a patient's heart. Until he performs surgery, he may not be able to observe this state, although past experience may give his inference a high level of probable validity. Inference is, of course, the very basis of scientific thought: what is important is that it should be distinguished from observation.

The traditional difficulty that psychoanalysis has had with this distinction stems in large part from a failure to recognize that the "interpretation" of behavior is inferential and not observational. If a client reports a dream of losing a tooth, then this report may be treated as an observation by the person receiving the report. If the observer decides that this is a "separation anxiety" dream, then he has made an inference. The dangers and confusions that arise when inferences are confused with observations is neatly illustrated by discussion of the symbolic significance of teeth provided by Lorand and Feldman (1955). Referring to primitive puberty rites that include the knocking out of the boy's tooth, they note that "the obvious interpretation of the initiation rite . . . seems to be that the operator is separating the young man from his mother, i.e., from the nipple [p. 157]." Shortly after this the writers point to the work of a fellow analyst, Rhan (1932), who had already concluded that there is a connection between thumb-sucking and dreams of losing one's teeth. The alleged connection was that, since thumb-sucking precedes the appearance of teeth in the developmental sequence of the baby, then dreams of losing one's teeth are really dreams about a happier earlier period—i.e., a wish to return to the mother's breast and suckle it as in babyhood.

Here we have an excellent illustration of the derivation of two contrary interpretations of the same phenomenon, i.e., losing one's teeth symbolizes the separation from the breast and also the return to the breast. Clearly, neither of these two inferences has any value as a contribution to knowledge until one or the other has been verified by the empirical testing of some additional consequence. For example, if it could be demonstrated that individuals who report dreams of losing teeth also exhibit other kinds of behavior resembling that of normal babies or infants, then we would have a theoretically provocative correlation. The superficial implausibility of the inference should not logically prevent us from testing it empirically, although it might lead us to spend our investigative resources dealing with more promising hypotheses.

THEORETICAL VERSUS EMPIRICAL SIGNIFICANCE OF DYNAMIC HYPOTHESES

Although the conduct of research aimed at testing theoretical propositions drawn from psychoanalysis has become less popular in recent years, many lines of research in psychopathology owe their origin to clinical observations drawn from Freudian writings. Selective deficiencies in recall can be shown to be related to the motivation of the subject, i.e., motivation may produce "repression." These findings are of enormous significance to psychology in ways that do not depend upon accepting the notion of "damming up libidinal energy" to explain them. Perhaps it would not be unfair to state that psychoanalytic hypotheses of a correlational type have been valuable in psychopathology to an extent that seems unlikely to be true of psychoanalytic theory.

The medical infectious-disease model and the dynamic-metaphoric model have both borrowed their concepts from other disciplines. Such borrowing is not necessary, and the next two approaches are instances of positions in which the concepts and terms spring directly from the measurement of the behavior of disturbed people.

The Statistical Model

Both of the previous models have envisaged the existence of some process that intervenes to produce the disordered behavior. Thus, either a pathogen or a misdirected energy source is invoked to explain the overt psychopathology. A radically different approach is provided by the statistical or mathematical model developed by some workers in the field. We saw in the first chapter that a model may be a kind of calculus accounting for observed empirical relationships in a purely quantitative fashion. Research workers who use such a model are mainly concerned to establish the mathematical relationship among various phenomena of interest and are less interested in explaining these relationships by recourse to inner processes in the person.

Various statistical techniques may provide the basis for such a model. One of the best known is the *dimensional* model advanced by Eysenck (1960, etc.). Relying mainly upon the statistical technique of factor analysis, Eysenck has developed several factors or dimensions that may be used as reference points for describing patterns of pathological behavior. Three fundamental dimensions in his model are *extraversion-introversion, neuroticism,* and *psychoticism.* Different patterns of pathological behavior can now be described in these terms and compared with each other along the dimensions rather than be seen as separate compartmentalized entities. In Figure 2-1, we can see the relative placement of the common neurotic patterns on the two dimensions of neuroticism and extraversion-introversion. Anxiety state, for example, is defined as high on neuroticism and high on introversion, while hysteria is high on extraversion but relatively low on neuroticism.

In fact, the most sophisticated use of this kind of model leads us to place individual patients rather than syndromes along the dimensions. Thus, an individual who showed elements of obsessive behavior and also elements of an anxiety state might be located in Figure 2-1 at about 0.4 on the neuroticism axis and at -0.4 on the introversion side of the horizontal axis.

In addition to these three major dimensions, several minor factors are used in Eysenck's dimensional model. The importance of the approach lies in this technique of placement of individuals along continuous dimensions rather than in discrete categories, and in the fact that this placement is based upon measurement rather than on classification. Common observation suggests that continuity of differences between individuals is more valid than discrete categories. Measurement repre-

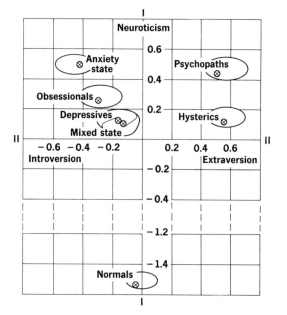

Fig. 2-1 *Illustration of a dimensional model in the study of neurotic syndrome groups. Here the two major dimensions are* introduction-extraversion *and* neuroticism. (*Eysenck, 1960*)

sents an advance over classification in any science, and from this standpoint the dimensional model may be regarded as a progression beyond simpler forms of classificatory model.

It should be noted, however, that factor analysis produces dimensions that may be plausible but not necessarily valid. The usefulness of this kind of dimensional analysis lies, as Eysenck has pointed out, in the fact that it may point to possible underlying variables upon which to base a theory of behavior. Thus, it may be possible to relate extraversion-introversion to dimensions of neuronal activity in the central nervous system or to particular methods of child raising or to some other independent variable. In this way a statistical model may lead the way to a biological or psychological theory. The validity and usefulness of the statistical model is ultimately demonstrated by its power to make correct predictions about as yet unobserved phenomena and not merely by its internal consistency.

The Behavioral Model

General experimental psychology has, over the past three-quarters of a century, accumulated a solid body of knowledge about the way in which the behavior of living creatures is determined. This body of knowledge and the concepts around which it is organized provide the elements of what may be termed the *behavioral model* of psychopathology. Strictly speaking, it is not so much a formal model as it is a point of view. If the several variations that may be found are ignored, the fundamental assumptions of the behavioral approach are that the behavior of organisms, including human beings, may be understood as the outcome of:

1. Past learning in similar situations.
2. Current states of motivation and their influence upon both activity and differential sensitivity to the environment.
3. Individual differences of a biological order. These latter differences may be determined either genetically or externally.

For the behavioral psychopathologist the crucial concepts are neither those of "disease" or "syndrome" nor those of "libido" or "id." They are concepts such as *reinforcement, punishment, generalization, perceptual threshold,* and *arousal.* Exactly the same concepts are in use by general psychologists who never concern themselves with problems of psychopathology. They are terms, in other words, that are part and parcel of behavioral science.

Among the important respects in which this approach differs from those already discussed is the fact that it is not an analogy. Neurotic responses are not explained by an *analogy* to the learning of "normal" conditioned responses—they are assumed to be a member of the class of conditioned responses. Hysterical blindness is not assumed to be *analogous* to experimentally produced narrowing of perception—it is assumed to be a direct example of the same process. Techniques of measurement and experimentation that have been developed in the psychological laboratory (not only those evolved at the bedside or on the therapist's couch) are employed by the experimental psychopathologist. As a result, many problems of reliability and validity have been solved long before the research began. Norms for the performance of nonpathological populations have generally been accumulated over decades. Technical requirements for control and application of these procedures are well-established, and hence the risks of some fundamental methodological error are much reduced.

Models and Reality

It is the business of a model to simplify complex data for the convenience of the investigators who use it. Simplification is always obtained at the expense of something else—usually at the cost of ignoring many aspects of the realities with which the model is supposed to deal. Although adherents of both the psychoanalytic and behavioral models agree that biological differences among individuals are significant factors in determining their later behavior, their models do not make any serious provision for biological explanations. This is particularly the case when the biology concerned is the biology of genetics. Indeed there are times when the omission of genetic considerations can be seen not as a sacrifice in the service of simplicity but as a reflection of strongly held objections to their inclusion under any circumstances. As we shall see later on, in Chapter 6, the omission of genetic principles from any model purporting to account for abnormal behavior is a serious matter. It is hardly an exaggeration to state that this kind of neglect weakens the claim of a model to the respect of other investigators.

Exactly the same strictures could be pronounced against purely biological models. The investigator who hopes to explain the complexity of schizophrenic behavior solely by reference to biochemical variables, for example, seems foredoomed to failure. Unfortunately, individual investigators easily move from a position of accepting a particular model as a matter of practical convenience to one of believing that the model is "true" in some metaphysical sense. It is then but a short step to concluding that adherents of other models are either incompetent or malevolent. When this happens we see the rise of controversies in the scientific literature marked not by the exchange of rational argument and counterargument but by aspersions on the motives and skills of the opponents.

We should not conclude this discussion of models, therefore, without reiterating that models and theories should be held tentatively and with full knowledge that they will rarely do justice to the wealth of phenomena involved in psychopathology. A conviction of the correctness of one's own hypotheses is a sturdy support in the hard labor of scientific investigation: it is a poor counselor when the time comes to consider the merits of rival hypotheses.

Summary

We have seen that work in psychopathology has been dominated historically by the medical model. More precisely this might be termed the infectious-disease model. This model has brought certain advantages in the care of the person suffering from behavior pathology. It has serious weaknesses in its current form as a vehicle for research. Chief among these are the problems of classification and diagnostic categories generally and their validity for either etiology or prognosis.

Another influential alternative has been the dynamic model. Here the major difficulties from a research point of view are the looseness of definitions, the lack of empirical support, and the methodological confusion by psychoanalytic theorists of inference with observation.

Nontheoretical mathematical models have also been applied to research problems. In this chapter, the dimensional model of Eysenck has been examined briefly as an example of one of these.

Finally, the applicability of the common principles of behavioral psychology (including the concepts of learning, perception, and motivation) has been indicated. This approach is seen as particularly useful. Its findings are readily integrated into psychological science generally, and the experimental methods and apparatus have reached a considerable degree of sophistication.

CHAPTER 3

RESEARCH TACTICS IN
PSYCHOPATHOLOGY

In this chapter we shall consider some of the major tactics available to the psychopathologist in the conduct of his research. In any presentation of research methods, one runs the risk of implying that investigations are always conducted in a neat, planned manner and that all questions of research design are settled before any data collection starts. Such a state of affairs would be ideal, but the activities of many research scientists scarcely accord with the description. They may work according to hunches, may develop their methods as they go along, and may be hard put to explain the rationale for their approach until the investigation is well under way. Nevertheless, it is possible to identify certain major tactics employed by psychopathologists and to evaluate the advantages and weaknesses of each.

At the outset, let us consider some general problems in the logic of research activities.

Exploration versus Hypothesis Testing

In one kind of research design, the investigator begins by deducing some specific consequence from a general theory. For example, we might note the theoretical proposition of Venables (1964) to the effect that subjects in the acute stage of schizophrenia suffer from low arousal levels. From this it could be deduced that, if the arousal level can be elevated in some way (e.g., by giving appropriate drugs), then some of the symptoms of acute schizophrenia would be alleviated, at least temporarily. This is now a hypothesis formulated in *general terms*, i.e., drugs that elevate arousal levels will alleviate the symptoms of acute schizophrenia. Investigation of this hypothesis requires that the general terms be made operational. In this case, making the terms operational would require (1) the selection of a specific drug, (2) the selection of specific patient populations, and (3) the selection of definite and precise ways of measuring changes in some symptomatic behavior. When all these decisions have been made, we have an *operational hypothesis*. Here, for example, we might decide that (1) the administration of the drug *methamphetamine* to (2) patients bearing a diagnosis of schizophrenia but with less than six months' hospitalization should lead (3) to a normalizing of their performance on a simple reaction-time task.

A very considerable proportion of published research in psychopathology is of this kind. Most of it is done in this way for one of two reasons. Either the research is conducted primarily to test a theory that already has some currency among psychopathologists or the "theory" is developed as a loose framework against which to view the possible results. This second use is actually only quasi-legitimate but is resorted to because of the difficulties attendant upon doing exploratory, non-hypothesis-testing research. Let us consider an investigator who is simply curious about "what would happen if" he were to manipulate certain variables in certain ways or who wonders whether there is a connection between one phenomenon and another. His "hypothesis" is very loosely held and may not even be verbalized in any overt sense.

An investigator who notices that he himself feels a little gloomy when there is a prolonged spell of winter rain may wonder whether there is any connection between climate and suicide rate in different parts of the world. Sheer curiosity may drive him to conduct the necessary investigation and if the results are positive (i.e., if there is a connection), then he has discovered an interesting relationship that may well provoke some theorizing on his part or others. On the other hand, if there is no discernible relationship, the investigator has, as it were, nothing to "report," at least in publishable form. It is difficult to report to the effect "Isn't this surprising; there is no connection between A and B" unless the investigator can establish beforehand some convincing hypothesis about a potential relationship that might reasonably have been expected to emerge. Our imaginary investigator might decide to report his negative results by beginning his description of the study with a reference to the well-established differences in suicide rates in different countries and to the plausibility, therefore, that climate is a variable, since climate also varies from one country to another. To the extent that he can make a plausible case for the "hypothesis," his results, either positive or negative, become reportable.

The crucial distinction between this kind of hypothesis testing and true hypothesis testing is that in the latter case the hypothesis is a *necessary* consequence of the theory whereas in the former case it is at best a *possible* consequence of a loosely formulated set of notions not yet integrated into a theory. There is, of course, no solid reason why purely exploratory research of the "Let's see what happens when" variety should not be conducted provided that suitably systematic development of any findings takes place. One leading psychologist has been moved to protest the excessive emphasis upon theory testing in the behavioral sciences as follows:

> Our current sophistication with respect to the design of experiments, statistically speaking, is a brilliant development of method without which we would be much better off. . . . No research gets done by the man who must do only the experiments that are beyond criticism. . . . There are schools in which research cannot begin until the student has a plausible hypothesis to test. This is unwise for it rules out the study which starts with the question "What would happen if I did so and so?" or with the feeling or hunch that there is something of interest to be found out in some particular area. A fertile investigation is more likely to end up with a hypothesis in testable form than to begin with one. The hypothesis, of course, can then be tested; I do not mean to deny that this is a part of research [Hebb, 1958, pp. 463–464].

Etiological Hypotheses, Definitional Hypotheses, and Therapeutic Hypotheses

For our purposes, it may help to distinguish among three general classes of hypothesis that appear frequently in the literature of psychopathology. The first of these we shall call *etiological* hypothesis. Such a hypothesis is one which states that some psychopathological phenomenon is the result of specified variables; these may be anything from a chemical toxin to a specific pattern of child-rearing practices by the patient's parents. This etiology may be either *necessary* (that is to say, if it is not present, the pathology will not develop) or *sufficient* (i.e., it will produce the pathology, but the pathology might be produced by other variables without its being present). In the study of the duodenal ulcer with which we began the first chapter of this book, the etiological variables of gastric hypersecretion and psychic conflict were both necessary but neither alone was sufficient.

The second class of hypothesis we shall term *definitional*. Essentially, a definitional hypothesis states that a particular psychopathological pattern or response is simply an instance of some more general phenomenon. An example of this hypothesis is to be found in studies that seek to demonstrate that schizophrenia is a form of brain injury by showing similarities in the behavior of schizophrenics and the brain-injured.

What is important to note here is that the hypothesis is not formulated so as to lead to a search for brain injury in the schizophrenic. The investigative observations all remain at the behavioral level. The aim is to demonstrate identity between schizophrenic behavior and brain-injured behavior. Generally speaking, the goal of this kind of study is to generate a *redefinition* of one of the patterns—in this case, were the results positive, schizophrenia would be redefined presumably as a kind of organic pathology.

A variant of this kind of hypothesis occurs when the investigator wishes to demonstrate that psychopathological behavior can be redefined as an instance of some simpler psychological process, even though the explanation of the simpler process may be in doubt. This would be in contrast to the preceding illustration where in it was hoped to demonstrate the identity of schizophrenia and brain damage. Such a demonstration—if convincing—suggests an etiology for schizophrenia because it is now defined as a subtype of a disorder for which the etiology is known. However, in this second kind of definitional hypothesis, a successful demonstration will not automatically bring with it some insight into the etiology of the psychopathology.

Let us consider an example of delusional thinking in which a paranoid patient believes himself to be the mayor of New York City. This particular pathology might be a subtype of any one of several kinds of psychological process. Perhaps the patient's real difficulty is loss of memory coupled with embarrassment about admitting to this loss and hence a tendency to make up answers rather than say that he doesn't know. Having forgotten who he is, he invents an identity, using any name that comes to mind. Perhaps the patient knows perfectly well who he is but gives delusional answers because it leads people to avoid him and gives him the isolation that he craves. Perhaps he has a fundamental difficulty in syllogistic reasoning and has concluded something along the following lines: "I live in New York City. The mayor lives in New York City. Therefore, I am the mayor."

The patient's delusional behavior may be an instance of any of these processes. Note that we do not understand the origin of these processes: we do not know what produces the loss of memory or the wish to avoid others or the loss of logical reasoning abilities. Nevertheless, if we can successfully show that the delusional thinking is an instance of one of these processes, then we have simplified our definition of the symptom.

Now instead of having to account for, let us say, the presence of both delusions and social isolation in the paranoid patient, we may concentrate our search on the etiology of the social isolation, knowing that the delusional thinking will be explained in the same way.

To repeat the point of the two examples: A definitional hypothesis may or may not have etiological implications, depending upon whether or not the redefinition is to be in terms of a syndrome of known etiology.

A *therapeutic* hypothesis is to be found guiding research devoted to testing the efficacy of techniques intended to change pathological behavior for the better. A hypothesis of this kind may or may not have a theoretical derivation. Its theoretical respectability is usually of less consequence than its practical validity. For reasons that will become obvious, this kind of hypothesis lends itself more than others to tests conducted by means of controlled experiments. Since such a hypothesis, by its nature, is concerned with the effects of some variable manipulated by a therapist, it is feasible in principle to apply this variable experimentally under conditions more controlled than is possible in the study of natural etiologies.

Proof and Confidence

When a theory focuses upon the presence of a physical pathogen as the etiology of a behavioral syndrome, then it is susceptible of rather dramatic forms of proof. If it can be shown that there is physical evidence of the presence of the pathogen in the bodies of all patients suffering from the disorder, that it is never found in control subjects, that it is the only detectable difference between patients and controls, that the disorder invariably follows when it is introduced experimentally into subjects (human and animal), and that the disorder disappears when steps are taken that are specifically aimed at the destruction of the pathogen, then we would have an ideal set of observations leading to proof of the hypothesis beyond reasonable doubt.

In practice, the psychopathologist rarely, if ever, finds this state of affairs. He may find a statistically significant difference between patients and controls in the extent to which they were exposed to a pathogenic environment (e.g., the "schizophrenogenic family") but he may not be in a position to be sure that environment had any specific impact upon the patients. He cannot create the environment artificially in the way that the biochemist can administer the physical pathogen directly to a volunteer subject. Hence, he cannot be sure that the environment is a necessary condition but may merely suspect that it is a sufficient condition. He may find that experimental analogues of the schizophrenogenic family, such as inducing confused communication in an experiment, produce something mildly analogous to schizophrenic thinking in his experimental subjects. He may find that cultures in which the family structure is very different from that in Western Europe do not appear to have behavior disturbances that resemble schizophrenia. As these observations accumulate, none of them provide unambiguous proof of the hypothesis, for each can be "explained away" on one basis or another. All he can do is develop increasing confidence in his hypothesis as observations are reported that are congruent with it. Because of the severe problems of control that face him, the psychopathologist must work mainly with broad ranges of confidence rather than with convincing proofs. In this he is no different from the lunar geographer trying to estimate the character of the moon's surface from relayed photographs, or the archaeologist reconstructing the history of a forgotten culture from shards of pottery and the position of buried bones.

SPECIFIC METHODS

With these considerations in mind, we may now examine the various methods used in psychopathological research.

Clinical observation. A clinician dealing with a particular patient may be struck by some unusual feature of the patient's history. Wondering whether there is a connection between this and the patient's difficulties, he may become alert to similar coincidences in other patients whom he has in his practice. Should he find these coincidences rather frequently, he may begin to formulate a correlational hypothesis of the form: "Precondition A tends to lead to disorder B." This is an etiological hypothesis of the crudest possible type since it does not specify the nature of the mediating links between A and B. Stated in this form, the hypothesis is susceptible of only one kind of test, namely a test for *generality*. It is necessary to test for generality because of the selective nature of the original observations. We do not know whether the clinician used a stable standard of definitions for A and B in each case; we do know that observations are very likely to be biased if they are made by a person who knows what hypothesis is under test (cf. Rosenthal, 1964); we do not know whether this clinician's practice represents a random sample of the people to whom he wishes to generalize. In brief, we have only a loose hypothesis based upon casual clinical observation. It is a good beginning point for formulating a hypothesis but is not a valid contribution to science at this stage.

Controlled observation. Casual clinical observation frequently leads to a next step—the introduction of control. This is done by (1) stating the hypothesis in operational terms, (2) ensuring that the method of measurement for one variable is not contaminated by knowledge of the measures obtained on the other variables, and (3) quantifying the relationship mathematically. Casting the hypothesis in operational terms is achieved (as we saw in Chapter 1) by selecting measuring techniques (interviews, questionnaires, tests, etc.) and establishing their reliability. Contamination of the measures is controlled by assigning different observers to the A variable and the B variable, and, ideally, concealing from both the nature of the hypothesized relationship between A and B. Quantification is usually a straightforward matter of application of the appropriate statistic, although it is important that the method of measurement be devised to permit adequate statistical treatment.

Provided that statistical analysis shows the relationship between A and B to be significant, we have moved from the initial casual clinical observation to a position in which the existence of an interesting phenomenon has been established clearly and reliably. Our third step is to develop a hypothesis to account for this phenomenon, the relationship between A and B. We may do so because we now know that there is a phenomenon worthy of study and not merely an artifact of a clinician's biased sample or methods of observation. Given the relationship of A to B, there are two possibilities open to us. Either A is a determinant of B or it is itself a correlate of some other variable that is the effective determinant of both A and B. Although it may be important to repeat this

kind of study to ensure the stability of the relationship in other populations and at different times, these replications cannot in themselves establish the etiological direction of the relationship.

The controlled experiment.   The essence of the controlled experiment in its simplest form is that the experimenter prepares an environment in which he wishes to make his observations, all variables in the
environment being held at a constant value except for one or more—
the independent variable or variables—which are systematically
varied by controlled amounts. Responses of a subject placed in this environment are then measured, and variations in these responses are related to variations in the independent variable. Although this description gives the fundamental conditions of most experiments, research in
the behavioral sciences frequently resorts to some important variations.
We shall discuss these shortly. First, however, let us examine the most
straightforward kind of experiment in psychopathology—the *experimental analogue.*

The experimental analogue.   It is sometimes convenient to begin a
research investigation into a psychopathological phenomenon by trying
to create it under laboratory conditions. This is done when the natural
occurrence of the phenomenon is hard to predict or when one wishes to
observe the influence on the phenomenon of some variable that may
rarely coincide with it under normal circumstances. Physicists studying
lightning, for example, may re-create many of its characteristics in the
laboratory rather than wait for a thunderstorm. A careful distinction
must be drawn, however, between experiments in which the phenomenon of ultimate concern is outside the laboratory and those in which the
laboratory situation is itself the main focus of interest. When the former
is the case, then the laboratory investigation is an experimental
analogue; i.e., it is being performed as an analogue to the natural phenomenon and it is hoped that the findings will generalize to the behavior of the natural phenomenon.

For example, we may seek to produce hallucinations in normal subjects by using drugs, sensory deprivation, or the like, in the hope of observing the relationship of hallucinatory content to the personality of
the hallucinator, and we cannot readily do this by confining our obser-

vations to hospitalized psychopathological subjects. Experimental analogues in psychopathology may be analogous at the level of the *subject,* the *independent variable,* or the *dependent variable.*

Subject analogues are created by using subjects other than those to whom it is intended to generalize the findings. Animal experiments, generalized to human beings, are instances of the use of subject analogues. The rat is assumed to be analogous to the man. Normal undergraduates used in studies of anxiety, where the intent is to generalize from these subjects to anxiety neurotics, are subject analogues. Independent variable (or *stimulus*) analogues are found wherever the investigator uses a condition that is not identical with that to which he hopes to generalize. For example, in studying the effect of electric shock delivered to the finger so as to understand the effects of legal punishment on the psychopath, it is assumed that physical pain of this limited kind is analogous to the punishments prescribed by courts of law.

On the other hand, an investigator may have established that imprisonment does not appear to deter the psychopath from antisocial acts, and he wonders if this is to be understood as a general inability to experience anxiety. To test this (definitional) hypothesis, he studies the effect of electric shock to the finger of psychopathic subjects in the laboratory. Here the shock is not an analogue of imprisonment. The investigator does not plan to extrapolate his findings to the natural habitat but wishes to establish that his *definition* of the natural habitat phenomenon is a valid one.

Dependent variable (or *response*) analogues arise when the behavior of the subject is presumed to be analogous to some psychopathological pattern in the natural habitat. If we create stress in the laboratory and then study its disruptive effects upon solving anagrams because we wish to understand the effect of panic upon complex activities by a pilot during flight, then we are using anagram solution as an analogue to the problem-solving behavior that occurs during flight. We are, of course, also using the laboratory stress as a stimulus analogue to the stresses of flying. If our subjects are not pilots but undergraduates, then we are also using a subject analogue.

The tactical use of an analogue is quite important is psychopathology, and we should understand both its advantages and its limitations. The major limitation of the analogue is that the extrapolation from it to the natural habitat cannot be made with confidence until the necessary direct study of the phenomenon in the natural habitat has been made. There is only one way to be sure that errors in anagram solution are analogous to errors in flying, and that is to establish empirically that the conditions which control one are the same as those which control the other, i.e., that they both obey the same laws. We should also note that one event is analogous to another only with respect to some specified dimensions. The white rat is analogous to the human being in certain respects. It has a mammalian central nervous system in the gross sense, but the distribution of cortical functions is not the same. Like the human being, it can be motivated by hunger and pain. Unlike the human being, it does not appear to communicate by speech. We can list similarities and differences of this kind, noting that the validity of a subject analogue between the rat and man is most promising where the investigation is dealing with a common system (e.g., hunger motivation) and least promising where it is dealing with a system that differs widely between the two (e.g., learning via olfactory cues).

Analogues are most likely to turn out to be valid when the intended level of generalization is very broad. Laboratory stress is more likely to produce a useful analogue of the general consequences of stress than of any stress in particular. Stresses of different kinds all have some common features, as we shall see in Chapter 5. They also have specific consequences dependent upon the kind of stressor that is acting. Laboratory stresses (e.g., rapid mental arithmetic) are, therefore, most likely to be valid analogues of the common features of all stress and least likely to be valid analogues of the local features of some other specific stress (e.g., prolonged exposure to arctic temperatures).

Experimental analogues are to be found throughout the literature of psychopathology. A simple illustration may be seen in Conger's (1951) study of the effects of alcohol on conflict behavior in the albino rat. Excessive use of alcohol by human beings is thought by many psychopathologists to be a form of avoidance of unendurable personal conflict. In this investigation, rats were placed in an experimentally induced approach-avoidance conflict. Some animals were then given alcohol as a "treatment" variable, and their avoidance behavior was compared with that of animals given only a *placebo* (an inert compound). The effects of the alcohol included a marked reduction in the fear-motivated behavior (avoidance) but no change in the approach tendency. Generalization of the results of this study involves extrapolating from rats to men (a subject analogue) and from running behavior in the laboratory conflict to human behavior in more symbolic conflicts in the natural habitat (both situation and response analogues). The alcohol used represents a direct application of a significant variable, and thus no stimulus analogue is involved at this level.

Correlational experiments. Under conditions of complete experimental control, the independent variable is manipulated by the experimenter. If this variable is a drug, the experimenter determines the dosage; if it is a painful punishment, the experimenter controls the intensity of pain stimulus, and so on. Drugs or painful stimuli might well vary in their effect with the height or weight of the individual subject. Subjects, in other words, may bring into the experiment certain personal factors that could increase or diminish the effects of the independent variable. Most of the time the experimenter cannot be sure what these factors might be. Hence, he makes sure that his subjects are randomly assigned to the various groups of his experiment. In this way he reduces the possibility that he may inadvertently wind up with all of his heaviest subjects assigned to the largest drug dosage or with some other undesirable *confounding* of his independent variable with some attributes of his subjects. If he is sure that certain factors might affect his results via confounding, then he may control this by assigning subjects matched on this variable to each of his experimental conditions.

However, there are questions in psychopathology which center on the relationship between a subject characteristic and an independent variable. For example, is the effect of an energizing drug more marked on an anxiety neurotic patient than on a normal control? Does psychoanalytic therapy have better results with very intelligent patients than it does with patients of below-average intelligence? Many questions such as these arise in research into disordered behavior. We should note that here the experimenter cannot create the independent variables of intelligence or anxiety neurosis. He can only try to find people who differ with regard to these criteria and apply his independent variable to all of them. Thus, strictly speaking, intelligence is not an independent variable in the sense that it is controlled directly by the experimenter. Nevertheless, it is used very much like an independent variable: its value is assumed to influence the value that the dependent variable will take—in this case the extent of improvement in psychotherapy.

However, the logic of the experiment is essentially correlational. The investigator will discover the *correlation* between intelligence and improvement after therapy. Some methodologists would deny the term "experiment" to any investigation of which the logic is essentially correlational. Their main concern is the fact that in selecting for a subject variable, such as intelligence, it is impossible to be sure that one has not also inadvertently selected for something else which is correlated with intelligence (such as socioeconomic level or physical health). Ordinarily an investigator will try to control these unwanted sources of confounding by matching his groups on as many of them as possible. Thus, the groups might be equated for age, education, income, health, etc., and the probability is thereby increased that any differences that emerge are genuinely due to intelligence. Unfortunately, this matching is not always easy, and even when it is done properly, there is no guarantee that the experiment is free from other confounding variables of whose possibility the investigator was not even aware. Nevertheless, the practice of matching groups in this way and the degree of precision with which the true independent variable may be controlled give this kind of study advantages not found in simple correlations.

An example of a correlational experiment is to be found in a study by Harris (1957). He presented male adult schizophrenics with a series of pictures projected onto a screen. His schizophrenic subjects were divided into good-premorbid and poor-premorbid groups on the basis of a scale of premorbid social adjustment. A control group of normal males was also used. The pictures projected onto the screen included certain themes representing mother-child relationships such as dominance and acceptance. Subjects were required to estimate the size of these pictures as well as that of two neutral pictures (a square and two trees). It was hypothesized that the schizophrenics would be influenced by the content of the pictures when making their size estimates and that the results for the good-premorbid would be different from those for the poor-premorbid schizophrenics. Some of the hypothesized differences were, in fact, found.

The status of good-premorbid versus poor-premorbid is a variable that the patient "brings" to the experiment with him. He is selected on the basis of a scale. The experimenter could not manipulate this variable directly but could select high and low values of it, as happened in this experiment. Logically the results demonstrate a *correlation* between premorbid status and size estimation. However, the content of the pictures was varied by the experimenter and hence constitutes the independent variable in this study. The combination of experimental control of an independent variable with the correlational nature of the findings constitutes an example of the correlational experiment.

Correlational techniques. Many investigations in psychopathology employ some variation of the simple correlational approach. Essentially, this approach consists of measuring two or more variables in a sample of a population and computing the mathematical relationship between or among them as a correlation.

Although the expressed purposes of the investigator may be described in various ways, the eventual outcome of correlational studies is always definitional. Multiple measurement of a very heterogeneous population may be used to provide correlations that will, in turn, lead to the identification of syndromes. Once these syndromes have been defined, the investigator may seek to elaborate the definition of any one of them by (1) hypothesizing some common characteristic that seems to be present in all or most of the measures that define it and (2) devising some new response measure logically derived from this hypothesis and correlating presence or absence of the syndrome with performance on the new measure. For example, if we find that it is possible to identify a syndrome to be called hysteria by looking at the pattern of correlations among a wide range of symptom measures, we might also hypothesize that the central feature of the syndrome is the response of denying the presence of any unpleasant event. We might test this in an experiment in which the opportunity of denial is presented and hysterics are compared with normals. If we find that the hypothesis is confirmed, we have, of course, simply added another "symptom" to the syndrome definition; we have not proved that all the other symptoms are caused by a prior tendency to denial of unpleasantness.

Although a correlational study cannot confirm an etiological hypothesis in any final sense, it can, nevertheless, play a significant part in adding to the confidence with which such a hypothesis is held. If a correlation that had not previously been computed is confirmed after its existence had been predicted from a theory, then it may strengthen the theory without reference to any causal implications in the correlation. For example, if we theorize that character disorders of the kind sometimes called psychopathy are due to a biological incapacity to experience anxiety, then we might deduce that severity of psychopathy will be negatively correlated with performance on an avoidance-learning task. Such a correlation, if found, does not demonstrate that the underlying etiological hypothesis is correct, but the investigator will be entitled to regard the hypothesis more favorably if the correlation is found.

For an example of the use of direct correlation of several measures where the correlations are predicted theoretically, we may turn to a study by Davidson, Payne, and Sloane (1966). They were concerned with the different predictions that might be made from two theories of the relationship between personality and conditioning. The first of these theories was that of Eysenck (1965), which postulates a general personality factor of conditionability, namely, that people vary in the ease with which they can be conditioned, and hence, we should find correlations among the acquisitions of different kinds of conditioned responses by individuals. The central basis of this factor of conditionability is assumed to be a factor of *cortical inhibition*. Cortical inhibition may be defined operationally by several measures, chiefly a personality test called the Extraversion Scale (ES) of the Maudsley Personality Inventory (MPI), by spontaneous fluctuations in GSR, and by the sedation threshold test.

An alternative account of the relationship between personality and conditioning has been proposed by Spence (1958) in which the ease of conditioning is a function of *general level of drive*—a level that may vary in the same individual from time to time but with a tendency for some people to be chronically high or low regardless of daily variations. Drive level can be operationally defined by scores on the Neuroticism Scale (NS) of the MPI, the Taylor Manifest Anxiety Scale (two questionnaire measures), and by the basal level of GSR. Thus, we have two competing hypotheses, each with its own set of operational measures.

A simple conditioning experiment was conducted with 40 subjects. Each subject received mild but unpleasant electric shock to the finger after a warning signal of an auditory tone had been sounded. Withdrawal of the finger and GSR responses to the warning tone were recorded. Results of this experiment showed that (1) the measures of cortical inhibition did not correlate with measures of drive level—confirming that the two hypotheses really were different and not merely preferences for different measures of a single underlying process—and that (2) the measures of drive level correlated much more highly and consistently with conditioning than did the measures of cortical inhibition. Thus, the data favor the Spence hypothesis rather than the Eysenck hypothesis.

In this experiment it should be noted that the final findings are correlations and that, since the experimenter did not create levels of drive or degrees of cortical inhibition, it is impossible to draw a cause-and-effect conclusion from them. Nevertheless, they tend to support one hypothesis more than the other and thus provide us with another piece in the total jigsaw puzzle of explanation of the relationship of personality to conditioning.

Temporal correlations in the single case. From time to time an investigator may wish to study psychopathological phenomena in a single case because the case is rare or because it occurs in some environmental circumstances of special interest. Conditions may be such that the investigating clinician can manipulate or record changes in an environmental variable and correlate these with changes in the behavior of the patient. In this way he obtains a correlation over time between the values of the independent variable and variations in response to it from a single subject; the method is correctly known as the *method of concomitant variation.* Statistical techniques for computing the significance of these "correlations" are relatively complicated, and many investigators do not report them. Experimental psychologists, especially those who have been concerned with the principles of operant conditioning, have utilized this technique for many years without benefit of statistical analysis mainly to demonstrate that a particular environmental variable does control some current response. As in correlations found in groups of subjects, the main problems of interpretation relate to the possibility that changes in both the environment and in the subject's behavior are consequences of some other variable. When the investigator has manipulated the environment—not simply recorded naturally occurring changes—this danger is considerably reduced.

Example. An example of the use of a temporal correlation is to be found in Metcalfe (1956). The investigator studied the relationship of attacks of asthma in a female patient to her interactions with her mother. An illustration of the kind of data produced by these observations is given in Table 3-1.

Table 3.1   Use of a Temporal Correlation Technique to Identify a Precipitating Stimulus (Contact with the Patient's Mother) in Producing Asthmatic Attacks in a Female Patient

Occurrence of asthma [°]	Days with asthma	Days without asthma
—	15	70
Within 24 hours of being with mother	9 (60%)	14 (20%)
Not in contact with mother for preceding 24 hours	6 (40%)	56 (80%)

[°] x^2 significant at 1% level of significance.
Source: Metcalfe (1956), p. 65.

From the table we can see the tendency for contact between the patient and her mother to be followed by asthmatic attacks significantly more often than on those days in which there had been no prior recent contact. The relationship is correlational; i.e., the investigator did not control the occurrence of mother-patient contacts.

For an example of the method of concomitant variation applied under conditions of experimental control we can turn to a report by Allyon (1963). He demonstrated the effects of a schedule of reinforcement upon the eating and weight of an obese psychotic patient. Although placed on a special diet, she had refused to cooperate with this arrangement and would steal food from the serving counter and from other patients. At the time the study began she was handled by coaxing and reasoning by the nurses, without avail. To eliminate this behavior, it was essential to remove the reinforcement she was receiving—the personal attention of the nurses and the successful acquisition of food from others.

A schedule was arranged in which all cajoling and pleading ceased. Whenever the patient was seen trying to steal food, she was removed from the dining room entirely. At the outset, her weight was about 250 pounds—a figure that had been constant over several years. In Figure 3-1, we see the effect of the new schedule as it extended over 14 months. In this case, the relationship between the independent variable (eating and attention) and the dependent variable (weight) seems clear, and since the independent variable was under the experimenter's control, the cause-and-effect nature of the relationship is quite plausible.

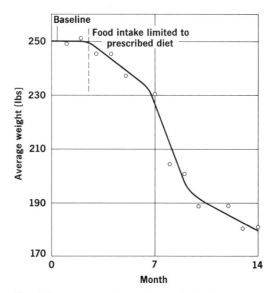

Fig. 3-1 *An example of the method of concomitant variation as illustrated by the use of reinforcement techniques to reduce the weight of an obese patient.* (Allyon, 1963)

Factor analysis. Correlational techniques also lend themselves to a specialized set of statistical procedures known as factor analysis. Although space does not permit a complete discussion of this method here, its essentials may be summarized briefly. If two measures correlate perfectly (positively or negatively), then we may wish to conclude that they are measures of the same underlying process or variable. Thus, should we discover that strength of grip, as measured with a hand-dynamometer, correlates perfectly with strength as measured by weight-lifting ability, then we might conclude that they both measure the same variable and we might wish to call this variable "strength." Since, in fact, it is rare to find perfect correlations among the results achieved by different measuring operations, we might find instead that our two measures (grip and weight lifting) correlate highly but not perfectly with each other. There is no mystery in such a finding. Both are influenced by some common variables but also by variables unique to each task. Their common variance may be explained by reference to a common underlying factor (still "strength"); but their unique variances may require resort to additional factors, such as practice at one of the tasks but not at the other.

We should be very careful here to note that the discovery of the correlations is empirically indisputable, but the decision to name the factors —or even to think in terms of underlying factors—is a tactical/theoretical choice. Existence of underlying factors cannot be demonstrated by the correlations themselves.

The major uses of factor analytic procedures are (1) to discover correlations with precision and thereby provide a basis for developing hypotheses about the sources of common variance and (2) to arrive at descriptive accounts of the coincidence of interesting phenomena, such as patterns of symptoms, with greater accuracy and objectivity than can be guaranteed from individual clinical impressions. We have already seen an instance of this latter use in our discussion on the validity of diagnostic syndromes.

Wittenborn's (1962) investigation of the intercorrelations of various kinds of psychotic symptomatology provides a clear example of this tactic. Using a sample of 150 male patients at a veteran's hospital, he obtained ratings of the behavior of each patient on 98 different symptom scales. Examples of the kinds of behavior observed and rated are:

"Claims can't sleep"
"Clothing discarded"
"Tics or grimaces"
"Fears impending doom"

From the complete set of ratings a master table of correlations was computed, indicating which behaviors tended to be correlated with the presence of other behaviors. Analysis of these correlations produced 12 distinguishable factors. Among these were the following, quoted here for illustration.

Factor A. *Schizophrenic excitement:* This included such behavior as speaking in response to hallucinations, general restlessness and distractibility, mumbling and shouting of vocalizations, etc.

Factor D. *Psychotic belligerence:* Including such activities as initiating physical assaults, deliberately disrupting routine, shouting or singing in a loud voice, criticizing others, etc.

Factor K. *Anxiety:* This includes delusions of guilt, fear of an abhorred act, distress caused by anxiety.

When the application of the same rating procedures to other samples of patients produces factors that are essentially the same as those obtained on the first sample, it increases the investigator's confidence that he has correctly identified patterns of behavior that have a consistent, functional relationship. Many of the factors reported by Wittenborn correspond to factors found by himself and by others working with different groups of patients. From this accumulation of data, he comments that "this study suggests that the present set of rating scales may provide a basis for the description of all the important dimensions of symptomatic behavior required by the various factorial studies published at this time [p. 128]." It is important here to note that the conclusion is a *description* and not a theory of etiology or a prognosis.

Unobtrusive measures. Webb, Campbell, Schwartz, and Sechrest (1966) have provided a thorough survey of what they have termed "unobtrusive" measures in the study of behavior. The essence of such measures is that they involve little or no manipulation of the environment in which the behavior is to be observed but depend upon subtle and ingenious methods of recording the response—or its consequences—in a fashion that will have minimal influence upon the response itself. Examples cited by these authors include the fact that the floor tiles around the hatching-chick exhibit at Chicago's Museum of Science must be replaced every six weeks, while tiles in other parts of the museum need not be replaced for years. This selective rate of erosion of the tile may be used as an index of the popularity of the exhibit. In this case, the response is standing and watching the exhibit, and the measure based upon the consequences of the response is wear of the floor surface.

To date, the major use of this kind of technique by psychopathologists has been in the study of documents written by patients. However, Wolff (1948) observed the movements of psychiatric subjects during meals and while at work. She reported that there were correlations between the clinical status of the patient and the kind or degree of gesturing used. Studies of written suicide notes have been made by a number of investigators (e.g., Osgood & Walker, 1959; Schneidman & Farberow, 1957; Spiegel & Neuringer, 1963) and a study of the spontaneously written letters of schizophrenic patients has been made by Maher, Mc-Kean, and McLaughlin, 1966.

The majority of these examples have necessarily used a correlational approach, with the attendant disadvantages that this method implies. Other problems are encountered, mainly the selective operation of irrelevant processes to bias the kind of data available. Letters from patients are usually mailed to the addressee, and so those kept with the records (and hence accessible to investigators) have some specific features that make it inadvisable for the hospital authorities to permit them to be dispatched as intended. Thus such letters may contain a higher proportion of complaints about the hospital or of bizarre communications than would be found in a random sample of patients' outgoing mail in general.

Against these difficulties must be set the enormous advantages that accrue from the nonartificiality of the situations in which observations are made. When the ultimate aim of research is to make valid generalizations about behavior in the natural habitat, this advantage cannot be overrated. Although many experiments in general experimental psychology may not necessarily have implications for behavior in the natural habitat, the psychopathologist, by the nature of his task, will always have these generalizations as his ultimate goal.

COMMON SOURCES OF ERROR

The possibilities for error in the conduct of any research activity are almost endless. In this section, we shall touch mainly upon the most common sources of error in psychopathological research. For the sake of convenience, we shall distinguish between *technical* errors and *tactical* errors. Technical errors will refer to errors in the technique or method used in the research, while tactical errors arise in the logic with which the research design is applied to the fundamental scientific question.

Technical errors. One of the most common sources of error in research in psychopathology is in the method of *sampling* subjects. By definition, the selection of subjects from a hospital population leads to the exclusion of those who are uncooperative or unable to cope with the requirements of the investigator's procedures. Thus, at the outset, most investigators are compelled to confine their conclusions to intact rather than to deteriorated patients. A further limitation exists in the kind of patients available for research in a large public hospital; they are generally of lower socioeconomic and educational level than patients treated in small private institutions, and these latter are frequently less available to the investigator. Within the public hospital—or indeed any hospital—the requirements of clinical treatment take precedence over research needs. Thus, the patient who is likely to be made available to the researcher is one who is not undergoing therapy of any intensive kind, one for whom a pessimistic prognosis has developed, and one whose daily schedule of activities is regarded as sufficiently unimportant clinically to justify making him available. Among the most prominent effects of this situation are the greater access to chronic rather than to acute patients and the concomitant problem of the confounding effects of hospitalization per se.[1]

Drug therapies.   These constitute a second problem for the psychopathologist. It is becoming increasingly rare to find any significant sample of inpatients in any diagnostic category who are not being treated with some kind of psychopharmacological medication. Since these drugs are commonly used to facilitate the management of patients, there is understandable reluctance on the part of many clinicians to suspend their use in order to make research possible. When this kind of cooperation is obtained, it is necessary to discontinue the medication for some period of time to ensure that the patient no longer remains under the influence of the drug. In many cases, the only solution open is for the investigator to record the dosage of drugs, variety, etc., for each of his subjects and include these as variables in his data analysis. Some subjects must have been free from drugs for this kind of analysis to be possible. The technical requirements for the proper investigation of drug effects are quite complex and not crucial to the question at issue here— the difficulty of getting nondrugged patients for research on problems unrelated to drugs.

[1] For a brilliant discussion of these effects, the reader is referred to Goffman (1961).

Control groups. These are a third source of difficulty. Besides the obvious need to match hospitalized patient subjects with control subjects on variables such as age, sex, education, and socioeconomic level, there is the additional problem of length of hospitalization. Matching for psychiatric hospitalization can be done only by using groups of patients with different diagnostic categories, but this excludes the use of normal controls. Normal controls are to be found by turning to subjects who have been hospitalized with some purely somatic disorder and who are undergoing treatment for as long as the patients with behavior disorders are. Even where this is possible, there may be reason to doubt that the environment provided by a medical hospital is closely similar to that provided by a large psychiatric institution.

Experimenter effects. Attention has been drawn in recent years to the *influence of the investigator* and his expectations upon the behavior of his subjects. We have already discussed the fact that an investigator who is strongly attached to his hypothesis does not make the most impartial observer of crucial data. Rosenthal (1964) has pointed out additionally that experimenters may unintentionally influence their subjects to respond in the way that the hypothesis demands. There are several possible safeguards against this: the employment of data collectors who are left in ignorance of the hypothesis at test; the maximum use of mechanical presentation of the experimental problem and the recording of the response; and the use of several investigators to permit the detection of biases that might be associated with any one of them, or the deliberate introduction of counterbalanced biases. This problem is not, however, peculiar to research in psychopathology; it applies to all research in which the investigator interacts with his subjects.

When the experimenter must himself act as a stimulus in the research, the problem of *ecological validity* arises. Let us consider the case of an investigation in which it is intended to compare the effects of a mechanical reward, e.g., a cigarette delivered from a vending device, with a "social" reward, such as a person's expressing approval, upon the learning rate of a group of psychiatric patients. If only one investigator delivers the social rewards by saying, "That's very good," or words to that effect, then it is not possible to know whether any results are to be ascribed to the power of social rewards as such or whether other personality attributes of the experimenter affected the outcome. For experiments of this kind, it is as necessary to have a representative sample of experimenters as it is to have representativeness in the subject sample. Unless this is done, it becomes dangerous to generalize about the effects of social rewards delivered by people in general, and the conclusions would be limited, strictly speaking, to the effect of the rewards delivered by the specific experimenter used in the study.

There is probably no limit to the possible errors in tactics that might plague the psychopathologist. We shall mention here only some of the major sources of difficulty. One of these is to be found in investigations in which the aim of the research is to establish that a particular kind of psychopathology is characterized by a *tendency to make a specified deviant response* in situations in which normal responses are technically possible. Should we be interested in demonstrating that schizophrenic language is *regressed,* i.e., that it resembles the language of normal children, we might decide to test this by presenting patients and controls with several pairs of sentences related to the same topic but with contrasting modes of expression, one typical of an adult and the other typical of children. We may ask the subjects to indicate which they think is preferable in each pair and may find that the schizophrenics pick the childish alternative more often than the normal subjects do. However, what we may have shown is nothing more than the fact that the patient group may be more prone to "error" of any kind; and, by limiting the possible error choices to those demanded by our hypothesis, we have predetermined the outcome. In other words, the logic of our original question demands that whenever we are investigating the frequency of pathological-type errors we make available to the patient not only the normal alternative and the hypothesized error but also several other kinds of error whose occurrence would negate the hypothesis. When patients are asked to select the most abstract meaning of a proverb, providing them with only an abstract and a concrete meaning may lead to the conclusion, based upon the greater number of choices of concrete alternatives, that they prefer concrete meanings. In the absence of other possible choices then, the only kind of error possible is the concrete error and the hypothesis will be accepted. In fact, these errors might indicate only a tendency to general error on the part of the subject. Had he had many other choices available, concrete choices might have occurred no more often than chance would predict.

This source of error is particularly apt to enter into research in psychopathology because the experimental populations are frequently marked by difficulties in attention and motivation over and above their specific symptomatology, with consequent liability to error in any task however low-level the skill it demands.

Much the same kind of difficulty may be found when the kinds of errors generated by a difficult task vary in their probability. For example, the Von Domarus principle of schizophrenic reasoning predicts that the patient is unusually prone to a particular kind of logical error—the error of the "undistributed middle." This is the error described earlier in this chapter wherein the patient reasons "I live in New York City; the mayor lives in New York City; therefore, I am the mayor." In fact, this kind of error is very common in the thinking of normal people also. However, normal subjects are less likely to make errors at all unless the logical problems are difficult to solve. By selecting a set of problems that is not difficult for normals but is for schizophrenic patients, it is possible to show that schizophrenic patients seem to "prefer" this error whereas normals do not. Clearly this conclusion would be unjustified unless it could be shown that patients seem to prefer one kind of error while normal controls make some other kind of error under circumstances in which both groups are equally prone to error. A good illustration of a well-controlled study of this effect is to be found in Williams (1964), who was able to show that the kinds of logical errors made by schizophrenics did not differ substantially from those made by normals but that schizophrenics made more of them.

A second tactical problem of some importance to psychopathologists hinges upon the *producibility of infrequent events*. Patients suffering from various forms of pathology often show considerable diurnal fluctuation in the visibility of their pathological responses. Many patients who have delusions are either unwilling to admit to them or are not subject to them all the time every day. Experiments involving delusional thinking are generally conducted to fit in with some other time schedule—the investigator's or one convenient to the hospital's housekeeping schedule. Consequently, the investigator is liable to get an underestimate of the percentage of his patient group who are subject to delusions. What he will get is an estimate of the probability that a patient diagnosed as delusional will be actively delusional during an arbitrary time sample. In other words, it is necessary to extend the observation period or the number of experimental sessions to a value that will reasonably encompass the time periods over which the phenomenon of interest tends to occur.

A failure to do this is often based upon certain conceptions of behavior pathology. These conceptions ignore the distinction between stable attributes of an individual and potential or spasmodic attributes. We might consider the difference between the meaning of "illiteracy" and "pessimistic" as personality attributes. A man who is illiterate is so consistently—not spasmodically—and his illiteracy may be demonstrated reliably at any time by presenting him with material to read. On the other hand, his pessimism may not be readily elicited by a manufactured situation and may refer only to a greater frequency of pessimistic statements than is found with the average individual. Schizophrenic patients are not behaviorally "schizophrenic" all the time—perhaps not even a major part of the time. Consideration of the temporal base rate is essential if research into fluctuating behavior is to produce reliable conclusions.

Thirdly, we may mention the problem of the *conceptual independence of the stimulus dimension*. Although the dangers of confounding variables in the selection of subjects are well recognized, there is somewhat less discussion of the confounding of variables in selection of experimental stimuli. For example, we may wish to study the effects of reward, punishment, and nonreward upon the performance of patients and normal controls. Were we to conduct this investigation by using a method whereby the solution of a multiple-choice problem would be followed by "Right," "Wrong," or no response by the experimenter, then we would confound the social-reward value of the comment with the information value of the comment. Thus a subject may appear to perform less nearly adequately under no reward than under punishment, whereas he is, in fact, being influenced detrimentally by the fact that this condition does not provide information.

All in all we can see that the essentials of a good research design involve so arranging circumstances that there are as few explanations of the results as possible. An ideal experiment is designed to permit only one explanation of the data—but the ideal is rarely approximated. However, the experiment in which at least one explanation of a phenomenon may be eliminated represents a significant contribution: the successive elimination of various alternative hypotheses by a series of experiments is the means by which most solid progress is made in practice.

Summary

In this chapter we have discussed the principles and tactics by which research is designed. Various goals of research activities have been described including the development of hypotheses for later test; the testing of these hypotheses via the experimental analogue, the experiment, and the correlational experiment; and the uses of factor analytic descriptions.

Some consideration has been given to common sources of bias and error in research in psychopathology. Notable problems are to be found in sampling and especially in the securing of drug-free samples of hospital patients. Observer bias, confounding of experimental variables, and failure to take account of temporal probabilities are among the more usual sources of error in investigations into disordered behavior.

CHAPTER 4

BEHAVIORAL PRINCIPLES USED
IN PSYCHOPATHOLOGICAL RESEARCH

In an earlier chapter we have described the behavioral model for the study of psychopathology. Investigators employing this model have turned to the basic principles of learning, motivation, and perception developed in the laboratory mainly during the study of normal behavior by normal subjects. These principles were not developed for the investigation of psychopathology: they have been applied by psychopathologists because they believe them to be useful in their work. In some instances the application has been simply the use of a laboratory technique, but it is probably fair to state that the major application has been of the assumption that the variables controlling normal behavior also control deviant behavior. By the same token, the principles that account for the former will have relevance for investigating the latter.

Examples of the application of these principles and techniques will be provided throughout this chapter, sometimes in conjunction with an example from the laboratory study of normal behavior and sometimes with the data of animal experimentation.

Learning

Learning may be defined as the process which changes the probability that a given response will be elicited by a given stimulus. The study of learning is largely devoted to the identification of variables that contribute to this process. These are sometimes conceptualized as psychological variables coming from the past experience of the subject or biological variables dealing with the biological factors that may modify learning. While the two sets of variables are in constant interaction, it is convenient to consider them separately for the purposes of exposition.

CONDITIONING

A fundamental example of learning is provided by simple *conditioning*. In what is called *classical conditioning* or *type S* conditioning, a stimulus is used that already has the power to elicit a specific and predictable response. This is referred to as an *unconditional stimulus* (US), and the response that it elicits is termed the *unconditional response* (UR). In conjunction with the US, the experimenter presents another stimulus, a neutral stimulus. This is neutral in the sense that it has no power to

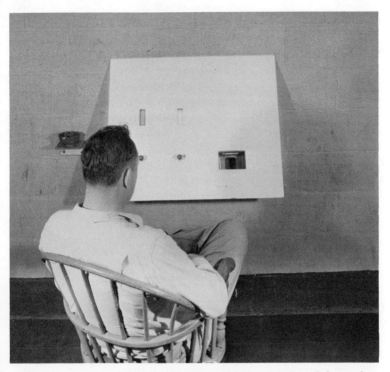

Fig. 4-1 *Operant-conditioning chamber used for research with hospital patients. (Photograph courtesy of Dr. Ogden Lindsley)*

evoke the UR. Provided that the pairing of the neutral stimulus with the US is done within certain temporal limits and sufficiently often, the former will gradually acquire the power to elicit the UR even when the US is finally omitted. At this point, when the UR is elicited by the previously neutral stimulus, the UR is termed a *conditioned response* (CR) and the formerly neutral stimulus is termed the *conditioned stimulus* (CS). The classic example of this procedure is given by Pavlov's technique whereby a dog is presented with a bell paired with food. The food elicits saliva, and, after a number of paired presentations (*trials*), the bell will elicit salivation if presented alone.

For maximal efficiency of conditioning, it is necessary to present the potential CS a little before the onset of the US—approximately half a second has been found to be maximally effective for some kinds of stimulus pairing, although for others the interval may be longer. There is also some reason to suppose that the CR is a somewhat weakened version of the UR—the dog produces a little less saliva to the sound of the bell than it does to the sight of food.

A second variety of conditioning is the process of *operant conditioning (type R)*. Here the subject is presented with an environment in which a particular response, such as depressing a lever, produces the unconditioned stimulus. A hungry pigeon may learn to peck on a key when the pecking is followed by the delivery of food. In this case, the food is the US, the stimuli associated with the testing chamber constitute the CS, and the pecking response is the CR. It is common in current learning theory to refer to the food, in both types of conditioning, as the *reinforcement*. In Figure 4-1, we see an operant-conditioning chamber used in research with psychopathological subjects. The lever operated by the subject is usually termed the *manipulandum*.

THE LEARNING CURVE

With each succeeding trial the conditioned response tends to increase in probability and magnitude and to occur with decreasing delay (latency) to the appearance of the CS. These three measures of learning may be used to plot the progress of learning. A plot of this kind produces a learning curve whose chief characteristic is that the *rate* of improvement is generally greatest in the early trials. As the trials continue, the increment provided by each one gets relatively less until the subject's response reaches a fairly stable "ceiling" or *asymptote* beyond which no further significant improvement is likely. Each learning curve found by experimental measurement will vary as a function of the subjects, the kinds of reinforcement, the nature of the response, etc. Hence, we can provide only a general form of such a curve, recognizing that there will be many empirical variations of it. Figure 4-2 presents a set of learning curves obtained in an investigation of the acquisition of a simple line-drawing task. The subject was required to draw a 3-inch line while blindfolded, being told "Correct" when his response was adequate and "Too short" or "Too long" when it was wrong, this latter information being accompanied by a mild electric shock to the wrist. This latter condition is described as a *knowledge of results* condition (KR). In this experiment the KR condition was terminated after the learning curve had begun to rise, with the effect that performance deteriorated.

Subjects in this experiment included normal controls (N), incarcerated sociopaths (IS), and incarcerated subjects without sociopathic diagnosis (INS). Statistical analysis of the learning curves for these three groups showed that the IS group learned the fastest under the KR condition. The general form of all three curves is, of course, the same, but the experiment illustrates clearly the variations in such curves that can be brought about by the selection of subjects, etc.

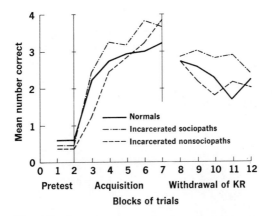

Fig. 4-2 *Learning curves for the acquisition of a simple motor skill (line drawing) with knowledge of results (KR) and after KR was withdrawn. Subjects were normal controls, incarcerated sociopaths, and nonsociopathic prisoners. (Persons & Bruning, 1966)*

THE PERFORMANCE RECORD

Once the asymptote of performance (under specified conditions) has been reached, it may vary with variations in the experimental arrangement. Variations in the schedule of reinforcement, changes in the total stimulus pattern, alterations in the motivational level of the subject, etc., may all operate to depress or elevate the level of performance. A running record of these effects is sometimes referred to as the *cumulative record*, especially by workers in the field of operant conditioning, where this recording technique is favored. We see an example of this kind of record in Figure 4-3. Here a psychotic patient was operating a manipulandum for a reinforcement of candy, but his responses were interrupted by his own hallucinatory behavior. This interruption depresses the rate of responding and is shown clearly by the change in rate on the cumulative record. Because of the nature of the recording chart, high rates of responding are shown by fast-rising traces (which reset themselves to the bottom of the sheet when the pen reaches the limit of the top), while slow rates are shown by relatively flat gradients of the response trace.

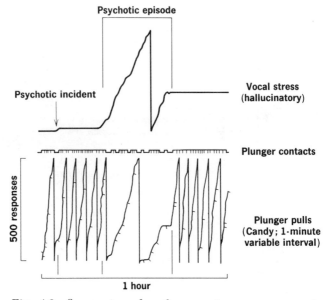

Fig. 4-3 *Suppression of performance in an operant-conditioning situation by the interference of hallucinations.* (*Lindsley, 1960*)

REINFORCEMENT

Although reinforcement is perhaps the most fundamental concept in current theories of learning, it is the most troublesome to define. A simple verbal definition has been provided by Verplanck (1957) as "the operation of presenting to the animal (or human) in operant conditioning, after it has made a response (and therefore contingent on its occurrence), a reinforcing stimulus or of withdrawing a negative reinforcing stimulus" and "in classical conditioning, the operation of presenting, contiguously in time, a conditioned stimulus and an unconditioned stimulus [p. 25]." Although the definition is clear enough, it does not specify what it is about any particular stimulus that makes it reinforcing. This is a property that can be established only *post hoc* by showing that its occurrence after a response did in fact lead to an increase in learning to make that response. Although it is possible to predict many reinforcements simply from common-sense observation of human and animal behavior (i.e., food is reinforcing to the hungry), we still lack any set of operations that will enable us to predict the reinforcing powers of a new stimulus when we have had no prior experience with it in a learning experiment.

Studies in animal learning have generally made use of *primary* biological reinforcements—food, water, pain-avoidance, sexual activity, and the like. Although these are satisfactory for the experimental creation of the conditions of learning, they are a limited sample of the many kinds of reinforcements that determine behavior, especially human behavior in the natural social habitat. In advanced societies it appears that variables such as prestige, success, and achievement are powerful reinforcers for much behavior. Some theoretical interest attaches to the question of the possible origin of these reinforcers as derivatives of biological reinforcers. Whether or not this is the case, it is common for psychologists to refer to them as *secondary* or learned reinforcements. For practical purposes this distinction between primary and secondary reinforcers is not of major significance. Behavior may be acquired and extinguished by either kind of reinforcement, and the general principles governing this acquisition and extinction appear to be the same for both.

EXTINCTION

When a conditioned response has been established, it may be eliminated by the relatively simple expedient of removing the reinforcement. This procedure is termed *extinction,* and its effects are gradual—the CR becoming progressively smaller and slower to occur until it finally ceases altogether. The speed of extinction and the shape of the curve of extinction vary with the conditions under which the CR was originally acquired, just as we have seen with the learning curve. Figure 4-4 presents the curve of extinction for a conditioned GSR acquired by human subjects to an unconditioned stimulus of painful electric shock. From this figure we can see clearly the continuous decline of the magnitude of the response as the extinction trials are conducted.

There is reason to question whether or not simple removal of reinforcement ever achieves complete extinction of the previous CR. When a response has been extinguished to an apparent zero level, removal of the subject from the situation for some time may be followed by reappearance of the CR when the situation ultimately returns, even though

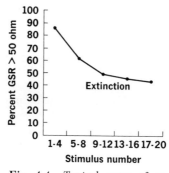

Fig. 4-4 *Typical curve of extinction, in this case of a conditioned GSR.* (*Dureman,* 1963)

there has been no experience of reinforcement in the meantime. *Spontaneous recovery,* the general term for this effect, has been observed widely in the extinction of many kinds of response. One major implication of spontaneous recovery is that the elimination of learned responses is very difficult to achieve—at least with any guarantee that the response will be permanently erased. Certainly, the elimination of responses solely by removal of the reinforcement is unreliable in this respect. When we consider that the basis of most psychological therapies is the elimination of maladaptive behavior and the substitution of some more effective pattern of responses, we can see the importance of a proper understanding of extinction. In the treatment of the psychopath, for example, it is insufficient just to make sure that he does not achieve reinforcement for some antisocial activity. It is necessary to establish some more adaptive alternative behavior by reinforcing it independently. A method of doing this is provided by the technique of *counter-conditioning*. By eliminating the reinforcement that has been following an undesirable response and providing a reinforcement for some more acceptable response to the same CS, it is possible to create a substitute nonpathological pattern. Thus, the child whose destructive behavior has been reinforced by parental attention may be handled by ignoring his destructive responses and by giving attention to constructive or helpful behavior. In this procedure the burden of elimination does not rest with the extinction process only but is supported by the creation of the counterconditioned response.

STIMULUS GENERALIZATION

Once a response has been conditioned to a particular CS, it will be evoked by other stimuli that have some similarity to the CS. The dog conditioned to salivate to one particular bell in an experiment will also salivate to other bells even though their pitch and timbre may differ somewhat from those used in the conditioning. This "spreading" of the learning is called *stimulus generalization*. Responses to a generalized stimulus are weaker than those to the original CS; the less the similarity between the CS and the generalized stimulus, the weaker the response to the latter. Finally, when the similarity is sufficiently minimal, no response at all may occur.

Degrees of similarity between stimuli may be defined and measured in many ways. Physical units may provide a basis for definition so that the quantitative measurement of wavelength may be used in defining the similarity between two lights of different color. Changes in frequency may be used to study stimulus generalization across the pitch of sounds, etc. When the change is measurable in physical units along some unidimensional parameter, it is customary to refer to *primary stimulus generalization*. In Figure 4-5 we see a simple curve of primary stimulus generalization to changes in wavelength by pigeons based upon an operant-conditioning procedure. Although the shape of the generalization curve is a matter of theoretical discussion, the general form of that given in Figure 4-5 is fairly typical.

However, in human behavior there is reason to suppose that significant generalization occurs across ranges of stimuli that are similar to each other in terms of their meaning rather than in terms of physical characteristics. Thus, a person who has acquired a fear of snakes may generalize this to include feelings of discomfort when seeing a picture of a snake, when reading about them in books, or even when seeing the word "snake." Generalization is often referred to as *secondary* generalization or *semantic* generalization when the similarity is mediated by word meanings or other symbolic representations.

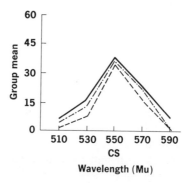

Fig. 4-5 *Gradients of generalization obtained to wavelength, the response being frequency of pecking by pigeons. (Thomas & Konick, 1966)*

Experimental evidence of this procedure has been provided by Lacey and Smith (1954). Using college students as subjects, they conducted a conditioning experiment in which the subjects were presented a stimulus word following which they were required to perform a simple motor task, tapping a telegraph key, for 15 seconds at an evenly paced rate. While tapping they were to chain associate to the stimulus word that had been used to mark the onset of the time period. Two stimulus words were used, cow and PAPER. For one group of subjects, cow was the signal word that would be followed (after 15 seconds of tapping) by shock; for a second group the shock followed when the signal had been PAPER. Presumably, since the shock actually occurred while the subject was thinking of words associated to the signal word, one group might acquire a conditioned fear response to words related to cow while the other group might acquire it to words related to PAPER. Tests of generalization of conditioned responses of heart rate, digital blood flow, and

GSR showed that generalization did occur to words related to the shocked signal word but not to words unrelated to it. Thus, subjects given shock after the signal word COW showed generalized CRs to words such as FARMER, GRAIN, HARVEST, but not to words that had no rural connotation. In this particular experiment, the investigators felt that they had demonstrated "unconscious" semantic generalization because the "conscious" association would have been between the shock and the motor tapping test.

A more direct application of the stimulus-generalization procedure to problems of psychopathology is to be found in a well-known study by Garmezy (1952). He used acute schizophrenic patients in a task that required the patient to move a lever when he heard a particular auditory tone. If he did this correctly a sufficient number of times, he accumulated points on a scoreboard marker that entitled him to a reward of candy. Under some conditions the subject would be punished by losing points for a response to a different tone—i.e., generalization would be punished. Under other conditions, a generalized response would produce no reward but no punishment either. In the outcome, the data showed that the schizophrenic group gave broader gradients of generalization under the punishment condition than normal controls did. Garmezy performed this experiment in part in reaction to an earlier clinical observation (Schilder, 1939) that schizophrenic patients seemed to react to everyone the same way—to fail to differentiate among people and hence perhaps among stimuli of other kinds. In this sense, Garmezy's investigation can be seen mainly as a definitional experiment: the etiology of the tendency to overgeneralization is not itself explained by the experimental results.

Stimulus generalization has several important implications for understanding human behavior. Because the generalized response is weaker, it is usually easier to extinguish a response made to a generalized stimulus than it is to extinguish one made to the original CS. When this extinction has been achieved, it, in turn, generalizes to other stimuli on the dimension and thus produces some slight decrement in the strength of the response to the original CS. By systematically extinguishing responses to generalized stimuli, it is possible to reduce the strength of the original CR to a level at which direct extinction becomes comparatively simple. We shall see more of this in our later discussion of avoidance learning.

Circumstances may be such that a response is not reinforced on all the trials in which it is made. When this happens, it is referred to as partial reinforcement. Partial reinforcement has several effects of interest to psychologists, but among them we should note especially the fact that this produces increased resistance to extinction. In view of the fact that much normal human behavior in the social habitat is likely to be reinforced partially rather than universally, it is not surprising that changing behavior is a difficult and tedious business.

AVOIDANCE LEARNING

Because of the importance of avoidance learning in the study of psychopathology, it is advisable to consider it somewhat separately from other kinds of learning. Furthermore, the conditions under which avoidance responses are acquired and extinguished have some features that differentiate these responses from simple conditioning.

Avoidance and escape. If we combine the presentation of a neutral stimulus with a painful US, two possible developments might occur. Depending upon the apparatus, the subject may be able to produce a response that will terminate the pain but that cannot be made before the US is applied. Such a response is termed an *escape* response because it enables the subject to escape the US but not to avoid it. Typical arrangements in animal experiments include an apparatus wherein the subject may enter a "safe" compartment by a door that is locked until after a US (electric shock) has commenced.

Alternatively, the interval between the CS and US may be sufficient to permit the subject to make a response that will get it to safety or prevent the onset of the US before the interval has expired. Thus, no US is actually experienced. This is termed an *avoidance* response. Avoidance responses are of particular interest to psychologists because, at first sight, it seems that they should be subject to continuous extinction. By its very nature an avoidance response prevents the occurrence of the US—and the elimination of the US is, as we have seen, the basic condition for extinction. In actual fact, however, avoidance responses are very difficult to extinguish. This may be due, in part, to the fact that the response has such a short latency that the subject does not remain in the environment long enough to experience the extinction condition. If we switch off the shock after establishing an avoidance response, the subject makes the avoidance response too quickly for the CS to be paired with nonreinforcement. In principle, to extinguish an avoidance response, it is necessary to restrain or prevent the avoidance response from occurring and thus compel the individual to have the experience of the CS and lack of US. Experimental achievement of this in animal research is fairly readily arranged, simply by preventing physical exit from the presence of the US. Human avoidance behavior in the natural habitat is less easily extinguished because the possibilities of restraint are severely limited. More important, however, is the fact that the avoidance response is probably largely mediated by the acquisition of the pattern of *fear* as a learned intervening response to the CS. Onset of the CS produces a group of fear responses, many of them visceral, which are aversive to the subject. Avoidance produces termination of the CS and termination of the fear. Termination of the fear is reinforcing, but the initial effect of restraint is to extend and increase the fear responses. Thus, any inadvertent restraint of an avoidance response is likely to lead to an exacerbation of the fear and to even stronger avoidance responses.

Avoidance responses are subject to stimulus-generalization effects, just as is the case for other CRs. Objects that have only minor similarity to the original CS will evoke milder anxiety and milder avoidance responses. The possibility then arises of inducing the individual to remain in the presence of the generalized CS and thereby obtain an extinction experience. Provision of strong positive reinforcement for remaining in the presence of a weak generalized avoidance stimulus thus opens the way to the eventual elimination of the conditioned anxiety to the original CS. Extinction of anxiety to a weak stimulus will itself generalize to other similar stimuli, including those that are a little more powerful. As they become weakened by this generalization, they can, in turn, be subject to the same kind of extinction.[1]

[1] Besides these difficulties regarding extinction, there are behavioral scientists who have suggested that avoidance responses are, in principle, invulnerable to complete extinction—perhaps because of differences between the neutral control of visceral responses and the neural control of motor responses such as bar pressing, etc.

A good example of this principle at work is to be seen in the practice of a kind of therapy known as *systematic desensitization*. Among many demonstrations of its use is that of Lang, Lazovik, and Reynolds (1965). Their first step was to select a strong avoidance response for study and modification. Fear of snakes was used (snake phobia), and the subjects were college students. Empirical assessment of the strength of the avoidance response was achieved by asking subjects to go to an experimental room and approach a live blacksnake in proximity and then to hold it. Strength of avoidance was quantified on a 20-point scale, with the response of holding the snake scoring zero and refusal to enter the room scoring 19. Other intermediate points were scored accordingly.

For subjects with a measurable avoidance response, an *anxiety hierarchy* was established. This consists of discovering the gradient of stimulus generalization of this fear for each subject. A graded list of items is ranked by the subject to indicate which is most anxiety-provoking and which is least. Examples are: "writing the word 'snake,'" "snakes on display at a zoo, moving in a glass case," and "accidentally stepping on a dead snake." Once this gradient has been established, the procedure begins with the least anxiety-provoking item on the list, i.e., with the weakest stimulus on the generalization curve. He is asked to imagine this situation (e.g., "a picture of a snake") while being instructed to relax muscularly. With an appropriate number of trials the item ceases to elicit anxiety, having now been experienced as a CS under conditions in which the anxiety response cannot occur (being incompatible with relaxation). Once this has been achieved, the subject can then proceed to the next most alarming item on the list, and so on, until anxiety is extinguished, even to the stimulus of holding a live snake. Using this procedure, the investigators were able to show a significant decline in the strength of the avoidance responses in their subjects but not in controls.

Punishment and behavioral suppression. When a response that is positively reinforced is punished, the consequences tend to be the suppression of that behavior rather than its elimination. In this respect the effect of an unpleasant stimulus upon a response that is being independently reinforced differs from the effect upon an otherwise unreinforced response. When a child burns his hand on a hot radiator, he is likely to avoid it indefinitely. However, when he is punished for playing with some attractive and forbidden object, he is likely to learn to suppress the behavior when the punishing agent is present but to perform it when the punishing agent is absent. When the source of punishment is removed completely, the original behavior will be relatively unimpaired by it.

Sometimes the only consistent cue for punishment is the behavior of the person who is punished. A child who is consistently scolded and punished for any behavior that seems aggressive will develop a fear of punishment whenever he finds himself beginning to engage in an aggressive act. Thus, situations that would normally provoke rational aggression in other people will come to provoke anxiety in this individual. Since there is no easy way to find an environment in which provocations to aggression will not occur, there is no escape from this kind of anxiety. Hence, the person may develop a relatively permanent conflict about aggression, perhaps severe enough to require therapeutic assistance in its solution.

Because so much of psychopathology involves anxiety, its development, and its domination of the behavior of the patient, the proper understanding of the acquisition and extinction of anxiety has played a major role in the investigations of psychopathologists. Many important aspects of this problem are as yet poorly understood. We are still unclear about the possibility of genetic differences in the ease with which anxiety may develop in people: the laws governing the conditioning and extinction of visceral responses are not fully determined, and hence the acquisition of the autonomic components of anxiety is more obscure than the acquisition of the overt avoidance response. Research into these and related problems is likely to be central to the work of psychopathologists for some time to come.

ROTE LEARNING

Psychotic deterioration is generally marked by disturbances in complex behaviors. Language, both written and spoken, is particularly liable to disturbance. Skilled muscular activities are frequently impaired; perceptual efficiency and motor coordination are often disrupted. Consequently, some psychopathologists have developed a special interest in these problems. We shall consider here the basic concepts of this field of specialization. In doing so we should note that there is no necessity to invoke special laws for this kind of learning—the underlying principles are the same as those found in the study of simple conditioning. However, specific apparatus and techniques have been developed in these problem areas and have begun to be used in the study of pathological populations.

Fig. 4-6   *Memory drum. (Courtesy of Ralph Gerbrands)*

Verbal rote learning.   A common method for the study of verbal learning is the presenting of a list of words or syllables in serial order. The subject must then learn the list, much as a child learns poetry by rote in the lower grades of school. In order to control the amount of time spent looking at each item on the list, and the number of presentations of the list, it is usual to employ a *memory drum,* a mechanical device of the kind shown in Figure 4-6. Because most subjects entering experiments on verbal learning already have extensive familiarity with words, it is necessary to control this by the use of the *nonsense syllable.* Verbal such elements as GIK and ZAL are compounded artificially to provide the necessary freedom from meaning in the creation of learning lists. Besides the learning of serial lists of words, *paired-associate* techniques may be used. In these, the subject must learn to respond to a stimulus word such as APPLE, by a response word such as CLOUD. The experimenter may vary the degree to which the stimulus and the response word are already associated in the language, an additional variable for control in this technique.

An interesting use of this technique in the investigation of self-esteem in schizophrenia appears in a study by Schooler and Tecce (1967). They hypothesized that, since anxiety is assumed to interfere with the performance of complex tasks, the learning of a complex list of paired associates would be impaired in anxious schizophrenics. Complexity of the task was varied by using paired associates of differing degrees of association. Thus, low-association pairs included words like WAX–MATH and BUBBLE–DRAG, while high-association pairs included BUTTER–DISH, FORK–EAT, etc. An additional way to increase the complexity of such a task is to introduce the factor of *intralist similarity*. This the investigators did by including pairs such as KNIFE–HAT and SPOON–FLAG in their list. KNIFE has high association value for the word FORK which appears elsewhere in the list, and thus there is created the possibility of confusion between words on the list which are not actually paired in the learning task but which have high association values in normal language usage.

Schooler and Tecce's data suggested that in regressed schizophrenic patients there was a significant decrement in performance following *favorable* evaluation of their performance! They interpret this to mean that, since the patients have such low self-esteem, any favorable evaluation tends to be disturbing and to increase anxiety, and hence produces interference in a complex task as expected.

Motor skill learning. Yet an additional kind of learning task is used in the study of motor skills. Here again no special principles are involved, but the emphasis is upon the acquisition of long sequences of movements, usually in response to changing stimulation. Driving a car, playing golf, and performing surgery are everyday examples of the kind of sequence envisaged here. Because of this complexity, the types of apparatus or task used vary enormously from one experiment to another.

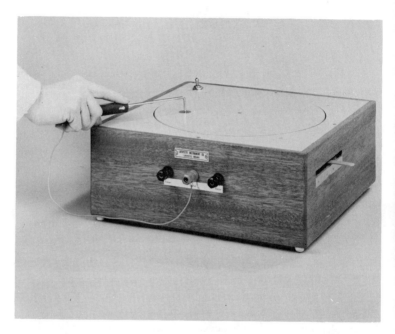

Fig. 4-7 *Pursuit rotor. The subject is required to keep the tip of the stylus on the small brass contact which moves as the turntable rotates. (Courtesy Lafayette Instrument Co., Lafayette, Ind.)*

However, at a relatively simple level, the pursuit rotor (see Figure 4-7) has become a standard laboratory instrument and has been used quite frequently to study various behavioral processes in psychopathological samples.

SPECIAL EFFECTS IN LEARNING STUDIES

From the vast literature of the psychology of learning, a number of important variables have been identified that affect learning and/or performance. In some cases these effects have led to the development of additional concepts to account for them. Some of the more important instances follow here.

MASSED VERSUS SPACED TRIALS

The interval between one presentation of the CS and the next may be varied and thereby produce longer or shorter rest periods for the subject between each trial. This dimension of long versus short is known as the spacing-versus-massing arrangement, massed trials having little or no rest period between responses. Overall, the effect of massing, in contrast to the effect of spacing, is to depress performance in a learning task. However, the depression of performance may dissipate when the subject is permitted to rest. After a rest period, the subject may begin performing at a higher level than he reached before the rest period, even though there has been no practice in the interim. A gain in performance of this kind is termed *reminiscence*.

Although there are other possible interpretations, reminiscence has been generally regarded as a consequence of the dissipation of *reactive inhibition*. When any response occurs, there is a very brief interval immediately following it in which the probability and the strength of another response of the same kind are reduced. This can be conceived of as the result of a temporarily induced state of inhibition produced by the effort of making the response (i.e., a momentary fatigue effect), though this inhibition dissipates with rest.

Since reactive inhibition has the effect of retarding the effectiveness of responses in a learning task, it is natural to wonder whether subjects who are slow to learn—such as regressed psychotics—are handicapped by unusually high levels of reactive inhibition. If this were the case, we should expect that patients would be much worse than controls under conditions in which reactive inhibition has a chance to build up. Under conditions of massed practice and after a considerable number of trials had been given, the difference between schizophrenics and controls should be much more in evidence than under spaced and fewer trials. Tizard and Venables (1957) tested this hypothesis, comparing schizophrenics with depressives. The former showed much more reminiscence after rest than did the latter, and this result suggests the accrual of more reactive inhibition, as had been hypothesized.

Learning one task may have an effect upon the learning of a later one. This effect may be to facilitate the acquisition or performance of the second task or it may be to create difficulties for it. Referring to these as task 1 and task 2, we may say that if subjects trained on task 1 perform better on task 2 than a control subject with no experience on task 1 does, the effect is *positive transfer*. If experience on task 1 produces poorer performance on task 2 than is found in the naïve control group, then the effect is *negative transfer*. Although the details are too complicated for exposition here, it is obvious that processes of stimulus generalization play a part in producing either effect.

SERIAL-POSITION EFFECTS

Where a learning task employs a serial list of responses—as in a multiple T-maze, a list of nonsense syllables, several stanzas of poetry, etc.—it is usually the case that the items at the beginning and end of the series are learned sooner than those in the middle. The literature is replete with examples of this, and one is shown in Figure 4-8.

This figure comes from the report of an investigation by Malmo and Amsel (1949). They were investigating the effects of surgery of the frontal lobe of the brain upon learning and retention. There was reason to suppose that this kind of surgery leads to greater susceptibility to distraction and hence that any kind of learning task in which there is a possibility of distraction would become more difficult for the operated patient. The serial-position effect is generally caused by the fact that items in the middle of a list have more surrounding distraction than items have at either end. Thus, any increase in susceptibility to distraction on the part of the subject should lead to a greater serial-position effect. As the figure shows, this is what happened in the investigation, the errors in the middle of the list being very much higher for the operated patients than for other control groups.

Remembering and Forgetting

When information has been learned, attempts to evoke it later may reveal some decline below the original level of learning. These decrements are defined as *forgetting*. Increases in forgetting are found in several psychopathological syndromes, including brain damage, hysteria, certain alcoholic syndromes, and so forth. It also occurs as a consequence of electroconvulsive shock treatment.

Before looking at experiments pertinent to this problem, we should examine the various ways in which forgetting might be produced.

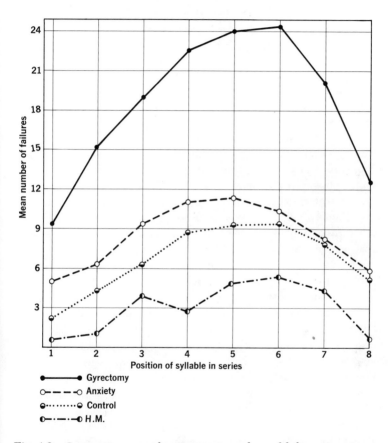

Fig. 4-8   *Composite curves showing mean numbers of failures at various positions in a list of nonsense syllables during learning by patient diagnosed as suffering from "clinical anxiety," brain surgery (gyrectomy), controls, and one gyrectomy patient who appeared atypical (H.M.). (Malmo and Amsel, 1949)*

Most psychologists would agree in principle that learning involves some process whereby the relationship between stimulus and response is stored and may be retrieved later when the appropriate conditions exist. Storage must, in the last analysis, consist of some kind of physical-biological change in the organism, almost certainly in the nervous system. Upon this simple statement several additional processes have been hypothesized. First, it may be necessary that the stimulus be attended to in order for the storage process to be activated—not everything happening to impinge upon the sensory receptors of an organism is noticed and available for subsequent recall. Second, the storage process itself may consist of at least two stages. There may be a preliminary temporary storage of information which may or may not then be "passed" for long-term storage elsewhere. During this temporary phase, disruption of the physical process may occur (a blow to the head or other coma-producing event), and thus the storage may never be completed. Once in long-term storage the information may be relatively impervious to disruption from physical sources.

Retrieval of stored information may involve the presenting of an adequate stimulus. For example, it may be impossible to get a subject to recall a name simply by asking him, "What was the name of the person sitting next to you during the lecture?", but the same subject may be able to recognize the name if asked, "Was it John Smith?". A series of experiments was performed by Cronholm and his associates at the Carolinska Institute in Stockholm (e.g., Cronholm & Blomquist, 1959; Cronholm & Lagergren, 1959; Cronholm & Molander, 1957). In a typical experiment, a patient who had been assigned to electroconvulsive therapy (ECT) was presented with a number a few seconds before the convulsion was induced. The number of seconds was varied from one patient to another, intervals being typically of 5 up to 60 seconds. The convulsion is accompanied by coma, and the patient remains comatose for some hours. On returning to consciousness, the patient was queried by the investigator, who asked him to recall the number that had been spoken to him. Memory loss was most marked when the interval between number and ECT had been brief. Memory was recovered as time passed but only up to a point. For example, three hours after the end of coma, about 60 percent of the 5-second group had recalled the number. At the end of 36 hours, this percentage had not increased. Their data generally support the notion that there is an initial temporary storage process which is vulnerable to disruption but that it becomes less vulnerable as time passes.

Turning from the rather gross kind of disruption produced by physiological interference in the initial storage process, we may examine the sources of forgetting that occur more commonly during normal daily living.

INTERFERENCE HYPOTHESIS

Much forgetting may be due to the fact that the initial storage process was subject to some kind of interference. The most common kind of interference is created by the presence of a competing stimulus-response link that is developed shortly after the initial learning has occurred. Thus, an instructor trying to learn the names of students in a course may find one of the several Smiths or Browns in the course more difficult to remember than someone with an unusual name. There are more instances in his past of the Smith name's than of the Pinchpenny, Leatherberry, or like names' being associated with various other faces. Interference effects may be reduced by narrowing one's focus of attention at the time of initial learning, i.e., by eliminating awareness of competing stimulation that might disrupt the learning process. Conversely, we might expect that individuals suffering from difficulty in maintaining focused attention would be unusually subject to forgetting because of interference.

If we examine this explanation carefully, we see that what is involved is not impairment in "retrieval" from storage of what was learned but inadequate learning in the first place. In one sense the "forgetting" is not a matter of having "forgotten" something but of having never learned it completely. An illustration of the implication of this for psychopathological research is available in a paper by Hall and Crookes (1952). They employed five groups of subjects, four consisting of neurotic samples, and the fifth, of normal controls. Initially, all subjects were required to learn a paired-associate list wherein the pairs had little associative value. Their performance on this task was measured in terms of (1) the mean number of correct responses on each trial and (2) the number of pairs of words correctly recalled on one trial but forgotten on the following trials. The experimenter read aloud the stimulus word, and the subject was required to recall the associated response. After his response he was told only whether he was right or wrong but was not told what the response should have been when he was wrong. Analysis of the data showed that the neurotic groups were significantly poorer than controls at learning the list but that they showed no greater forgetting of what was learned from trial to trial. The investigators concluded that the neurotic patients were subject to many fluctations of attention which impaired learning but which left the process of recall relatively untouched. Much the same explanation is possible in considering the results of the Malmo and Amsel study presented in Figure 4-8. Here also we see that serial-position effects are due to interference and that this interference is high in anxious patients—although not as marked as in the brain-operated group.

CHANGED CUES

Often in daily life we try to recall events under circumstances that differ substantially from those under which they were first learned. Thus, although the information may be stored, the stimulus presented may be inadequate to retrieve it.

AVOIDANCE OF RECALL

There is experimental evidence to support the view that some forgetting may be a matter of avoidance of thinking about an unpleasant experience. In general, the data indicate that when the event to be recalled is in some way injurious to the subject's self-esteem then recall is impaired. Events that were unpleasant in other ways, e.g., the recall of a simple physical injury, do not appear to be especially unavailable to memory. Here forgetting may be seen as the outcome of an active tendency not to recall—it is an avoidance response like any other avoidance response. Under circumstances in which overt recall of this kind is likely to be greeted with sympathy rather than rejection (e.g., during psychotherapy), the extent of forgetting may diminish dramatically.

An experimental illustration of the avoidance of recall ("motivated forgetting") is available in the work of Gossett (1964). He used two

groups of subjects, one comprising people for whom repression was believed to be a primary psychological response to threat and the other
including subjects who did not repress. Subjects were selected on the
basis of a personality scale. Each subject was then required to learn a list
of 12 nonsense syllables. Part way through the learning of this list they
were given a "test" described as a measure of personality and intelligence but, in fact, merely used to generate an artificial failure for one-
half of each group. Various parts of this test were subtitled with the nonsense syllables taken from the list to be learned, the syllables thereby
being associated with a failure experience for the subjects who were told
that their performance on the test was inadequate.

Following this, all subjects were asked to recall the 12 nonsense
syllables. The repressors who had been given the failure experience
were significantly impaired in their recall: their forgetting was presumably motivated by the unpleasant association between syllables on the
list and the experience of failure.

INCOMPATIBILITY WITH COGNITIVE ORGANIZATION

Quite apart from their pleasant or unpleasant qualities, some events
may appear to us as incongruous. An individual whom we have always
considered to be straitlaced and puritanical may be observed in a very
uninhibited activity, a student who has generally made poor marks may
do astonishingly well in a course, or a person who has always been our
enemy does us an unexpected kindness. Incongruities of this sort tend to
produce certain kinds of reactions from the observer. One of them is to
"explain away" the inconsistency so that it does not appear so inconsis-
tent: our straitlaced friend must have been temporarily under the influence of alcohol, the course the student took must have been a very easy
one, our erstwhile enemy was trying to get us to lower our guard.

Another common development is the forgetting of the incongruent
events. An experiment by Zimmerman and Bauer (1956) illustrates
neatly how our expectations about a situation determine what will be
recalled about it. They presented subjects with the task of preparing a
speech to be given either pro or con the matter of raising teachers' sal-
aries. Subjects were told that they would be addressing an audience
predominantly favorable (or, in another group of subjects, predominantly unfavorable) to the issue. All subjects were given sets of state-

ments both for and against the issue and some days later were asked to recall as many of the statements as possible. Each group tended to forget those statements that were incongruous with the nature of their expected audience.

When we consider the extent to which psychopathologists are compelled to rely on a patient's or parent's recall of events that may have happened years earlier in the patient's life, we can imagine the sources of error that this kind of forgetting may generate.

In this section we have, necessarily, confined ourselves to a brief and somewhat simplified version of the major principles of the psychology of learning. The serious student will wish to turn to more nearly complete sources for his advanced studies. Some of these are listed at the end of the book.

Sensation and Perception

Psychopathologists have paid much attention to sensory and perceptual processes. Complaints of perceptual peculiarities are common in schizophrenia and are found in other pathological syndromes. In this section we shall review some of the basic methods and concepts in the psychology of sensation and perception.

SENSATION

The sensory threshold. Any stimulus may vary in intensity. At low levels of intensity there may be values of the stimulus that are higher than zero, measurable with suitable physical meters, but not detectable by a human subject. The value of a stimulus that marks the transition from no response (too low to detect) to some response (just detectable) is known as the *absolute threshold*. Once the stimulus has reached the value for the absolute threshold, we find that very small increments in intensity may not be detected as increments. In order for an increase to be detected, it must be higher than the previous value by some amount that is then defined as the *differential threshold*. Relationships between the physical magnitudes of stimuli and their psychological consequences in the sensory system are part of the domain of *psychophysics*.

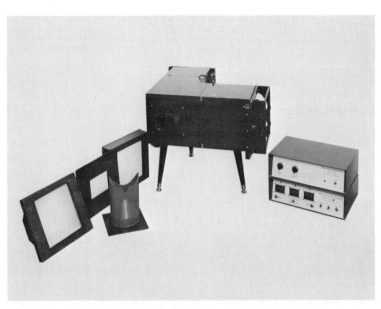

Fig. 4-9 *Model T-2B-1 Harvard Tachistoscope, including interval timers, and various stimulus display frames. (Courtesy of Ralph Gerbrands)*

Thresholds may be computed for any stimulus dimension, whether a simple physical one or a recognition of meaning.

Recognition thresholds are often calculated for stimuli that have verbal or symbolic meaning. A common method employs brief exposures of the stimuli concerned by means of a *tachistoscope* (see Figure 4-9). Tachistoscopes are constructed to permit exposure of a visual stimulus for very brief periods of time frequently controllable to 1/1,000 second. Investigations into questions of the special sensitivity or insensitivity of the subject to certain classes of stimuli are generally based upon a comparison of the threshold for recognition of the experimental stimuli with that for other, neutral stimulus material.

Flicker fusion thresholds. When a light is flashed on and off with some regular-period interval, it will be seen as a flashing light, provided that the oscillation of the "on" and "off" periods is sufficiently slow. As the rate of flashing is speeded, the flashing will gradually change until it is experienced as a fixed light source emitting no apparent oscillation. The point at which flicker fuses into a steady light is termed the *critical flicker frequency* (CFF). Values of the CFF are sensitive to change in the intensity of the light, the ratio of on/off in the flicker periods, and other physical variables. They are also sensitive to various kinds of pathology of the central nervous system and thus have gained a place in the research techniques of the psychopathologist.

Determination of thresholds with human subjects generally rests upon verbal reports issued by the subject. Individual subjects differ regarding the standard they apply when trying to resolve a doubtful judgment. Some subjects will not report that a stimulus has changed until they feel absolutely sure that it has done so. Others will report a change if they have any inkling that it might have done so. Naturally the thresholds of subjects who are cautious will tend to be higher than those of subjects who are quick to judge that a change has occurred.

Clark, Brown, and Rutschmann (1967) report an interesting experiment in which they were able to examine differences in the CFF of schizophrenic patients and normal controls by a method that permits the separation of actual threshold processes from differences in judging standards. In one part of their procedure, the subject was forced to state which one of four lights, seen in succession, was most likely to have been flickering. This method, in which the subject was not permitted to resolve a doubt by deciding that there had been no flicker, was compared with the traditional "yes-no" method. Results gained in this study suggested that there were no differences in the true threshold (defined by the forced-choice method) but that there were differences in guessing standards in the other psychophysical methods, the patients being the most cautious and hence seeming to have higher thresholds.

Apparent-movement threshold. When two separate light sources placed close to each other are flashed on and off in alternating periods, the subject may experience them as one light "moving" from one lamp to the other. News "tapes" produced by combinations of light bulbs on a display board over a public building give the impression of words moving along the board, an effect achieved by selecting the right on/off periods and the correct proximity of one lamp to the next. If the distance is too great and/or the on/off period too slow, the effect of apparent movement is lost. Here again we can compute a threshold for the perception of apparent movement by varying the on/off period until we find the value at which the effect is just obtained. This technique has also been applied to investigation of psychopathological patients those with organic disease (e.g., Saucer, 1958).

PERCEPTION

Many sensory processes, especially those involved with the reception of meaningful stimuli, are subject to distortion. These distortions are generally in the form of a compromise between the dimensions of the physical stimulus itself on the one hand and the effects of past experience and current motive states of the perceiver on the other. One of the simplest examples of this is to be seen in the phenomenon of perceptual *constancy*.

Constancy. Familiar objects are seen under many conditions of distance, illumination, angle of perspective, and the like. These variations in condition have striking effects upon the true physical attributes of the object. For example, the light emitted from a white object such as a plate may vary from dark gray (under conditions of low lighting) to brilliant white in open sunshine. By contrast, a piece of coal may be light gray under conditions of bright illumination and jet black only under very low lighting. The ability to perceive colors as they are under varying circumstances is one of the essential skills of a painter. When we ask a normal subject to match the whiteness of a plate under low illumination with some variable source of color on the white-black dimension, we find that the whiteness picked out to match the plate is whiter than the plate actually is under those conditions. In other words, the subject is influenced by what he knows to be the "true" color of the object and sees it as whiter than it really is at that moment. This kind of distortion is termed *color constancy*. Constancies may be found also in the perception of size, distance, and so forth. For any given set of observing conditions we may compute the average constancy, that is to say, the amount of distortion produced by the average of a group of subjects. Distortions greater than this are termed *overconstancy*, while a tendency not to distort at all, or less than average, is called *underconstancy*.

Constancy values are affected by many kinds of variables. Of particular interest to psychopathologists is the effect of the *narrowing of attention*. If a stimulus is shown to normal subjects with no cues present as to what the object is, the constancy effect is likely to be reduced or disappear. For example, the subject may be asked to view a white surface through a narrow viewing tube, being thereby prevented from finding that the white surface belongs to a plate. Under these circumstances he will tend to match it with a degree of whiteness that is truer to what actually exists at the time. By concentrating attention on a very limited aspect of the stimulus field, the viewer is in a situation akin to using a narrow tube. He is unaware of surrounding cues and hence tends to produce underconstancy. By the same token, excessively wide attention to cues in the environment will produce overconstancy. The study of constancies is, therefore, important in investigations of psychopathologies in which attentional anomalies are suspected.

Motivation and perception. Perception is influenced by the motivational state of the perceiver in two rather striking ways. First, the presence of a strong drive will lead to selective sensitivity to certain classes of object. For example, the hungry man is especially alert to the aroma of cooking. This selectivity appears to be accompanied by a narrowing of attention—a phenomenon that generally occurs in states of heightened drive. Second, it will change the perceived characteristics of stimuli so as to make them more relevant to the dominant drive. When the motive is an avoidant one, the effect upon perception may be to produce selective inattention to the fear-producing stimuli. Thus, the subject who is asked to recognize stimuli presented to him by a tachistoscope may find it harder to recognize threatening than neutral stimuli. This particular effect is termed *perceptual defense*, and, although an adequate explanation of it involves more than simple motivational variables, the effects of drive are quite marked in producing it.

A simple example of motivational influences upon perception may be found in the study of size judgment conducted by Harris (1957) and described in Chapter 3.

Perception and previous experience. The perception of stimuli, especially under conditions that are not favorable to accuracy (e.g., brief exposure or poor illumination) may be improved by experience with the stimuli beforehand. Although there are several experiments on this topic, a good illustration is to be found in the study of Solomon and Postman (1952). They were able to demonstrate that the threshold for recognition of nonsense words presented tachistoscopically was significantly lower for words that had been practiced previously under normal viewing conditions than for words that had not been seen before.

Perceptual defense. We have already noted that the recall of unpleasant events may be less accurate than the recall of neutral events. There is some reason to believe that the perception of unpleasant events may operate in such a way as to prevent their being recognized or attended to accurately. Perceptual defense, a concept developed in relation to this phenomenon, implies a tendency to defend against the perception of threatening stimuli. It may be seen as a special instance of the tendency of motivational states to influence perception. Eriksen and Browne (1956), for example, have shown that the tachistoscopic recognition of words associated with failure at an anagram-solving task was poorer than that of words that were neutral. It should be noted, however, that there is evidence to suggest that this tendency is itself a function of certain personality attributes in the observer—not all subjects exhibit the perceptual-defense effect.

Experimental data of Byrne (1964) reveal that some people are more sensitive to the perception of threat than they are to the perception of neutral stimuli—a reversal of perceptual defense. Byrne has developed a scale to measure this tendency (Byrne's Repression-Sensitization Scale) and has been able to show that sensitizers show a wide range of behaviors including lower threshold for the perception of threat, greater recall of unpleasant events, greater overt anxiety under stress, and the like.

Motivation

Our discussions of learning and perception have already introduced us to the effects of motivational variables upon a number of response systems. However, certain other important aspects of motivational influences upon behavior have not yet been described and we shall deal with them here.

By fantasy we refer here to the sequences of thought and imagery that occur in a person when the immediate determinants appear to have little to do with the current external environment. Although dreaming is probably the clearest example of fantasy, waking fantasy is quite common and has been the subject of much investigation in terms of the motivational influences operating on it. Since there is considerable reason for the psychopathologist to suppose that fantasy processes are crucial in some kinds of behavior disorder, the study of the factors governing fantasy is of some interest.

Experimental procedures designed to investigate fantasy have generally involved the creation of a motive state (e.g., hunger, fear) and the presenting of some stimulus that will generate chains of fantasy responses. Thus, hungry subjects were shown pictures, some of which had food-relevant content such as a restaurant. The investigators (Atkinson & McClelland, 1948) then elicited stories about these pictures and were able to show that with increasing hours of hunger there was an increase in references to hunger in these stories. Similar findings have been shown for a variety of other motive states.

MOTIVATION AND EFFICIENCY

With an increase in motivation there is usually an increase in behavior related to the motive. Responses reinforced by food become more rapid and more energetic when the subject is hungry. However, this relationship of motive strength to behavioral efficiency seems to be curvilinear, so that in very high states of motivation there is often a decline in the organized occurrence of the reinforced response. There are several possible explanations of this effect. One explanation supposes that with high states of drive there is a reappearance of irrelevant interfering responses that had been extinguished in the earlier learning to the point that they would not normally appear. Extremely high motive states may counteract the inhibitory effects of extinction and thus lead to their reappearance and consequent disruption of the normally efficient response pattern. Alternatively, the effect of high drive may be explained in terms of the narrowed attention it produces and the difficulty of producing adaptive complex responses which require the ability to attend to many changing aspects of a stimulus field.

Whatever the explanation, the empirical phenomenon is well established and is of interest in our understanding of the disorganized behavior sometimes seen in psychosis and in acute anxiety states. White (1956), for example, cites the behavior of intense fear in the combat soldier: "Scarcely aware of what he is doing [he] . . . may rush wildly about, laughing, crying, shouting in rapid succession. These reactions sometimes lasted many days in soldiers exposed to prolonged fire . . . ." (p. 208) The disorganized and confused behavior found in some states of pathological excitement such as mania and catatonic schizophrenia shows strong resemblances to this condition.

Summary

In this chapter we have considered in some detail the essential elements of the behavioral model for the study of psychopathology. Principles of learning, as evidence both in conditioning and in rote learning, provide a central theme. We have seen in many cases how direct investigation of the processes of learning in patients may throw important light on pathologies both psychological and organic. Sensory and perceptual systems are also important, especially in view of the fact that complaints of sensory and perceptual alterations often form part of psychopathological syndromes, even where no obvious organic pathology is present.

Motivational influences upon perception and recall efficiency are clearly significant in producing anomalies, deficits, and other changes in a wide range of behavior. Learning, perception, and motivation all interact in the actual behavior of real patients, and their division into subtopics in this chapter should not obscure the fact that any pattern of psychopathology can be properly understood only with reference to this interaction. The role of biological variables in this interaction has been postponed to the following chapter. It is to these that we shall now turn.

CHAPTER 5

BIOPSYCHOLOGICAL SYSTEMS
IN PSYCHOPATHOLOGY

All the effects of the environment, all the learning experiences, and all the motivational states we have discussed so far occur to individuals with particular biological characteristics. The human being is not an "empty" organism or a "black box" whose behavior can be comprehensively described without reference to his biology. For particular purposes it may be possible to proceed without regard to biological factors. Studies of the effects on learning of one kind of reinforcement, for example, versus another may be conducted without need for detailed consideration of the inner workings by which reinforcements come to affect behavior, and so on.

However, the psychopathologist must be continually mindful of the fact that direct biological aberration may produce behavioral aberration. Hence, any behavioral aberration *may* be incomprehensible if studied only in terms of environmental forces that operated on the individual. Disordered emotional patterns are so prominent in psychopathology, and emotional expression is, in turn, so much a reflection of the functioning of the visceral nervous system that any attempt to understand deviant emotions without an understanding of visceral nervous functioning is doomed to naïveté. In many instances, especially in the psychosomatic disorders, the major symptom may be bodily malfunctioning. Research into environmental influences upon psychosomatic patterns can hardly go forward without an intelligent grasp of the kind of malfunctioning under scrutiny.

Finally, we note that the behavioral consequences of known bodily pathology are an important area of study by many psychopathologists. Brain damage, intoxication, aging, and endocrine disorders are some of the most common conditions producing aberrant behavior. Here again, an understanding of the origin of this behavior and the development of ways to change it can hardly proceed in ignorance of the underlying biology of the condition concerned.

Stress

One of the most important unifying concepts in the relationship between biology and behavior disorder is that of *stress*. We talk about the stresses of living and the stresses caused by certain kinds of parental interaction; we saw in Chapter 1 that service in an Army recruit-training center was assumed to provide stress. The range of environmental events described as stressors is very wide—so wide, in fact, that no common factors in the situations have been found that we might point to as the "essence" of a stress stimulus. Individual differences in what is stressful are great and constitute a powerful source of variability. Instead, most attention has been paid to the fact that this range of situations has in common a particular set of biological consequences upon the individual exposed to them. Thus, we might define stressors as those situations that produce a pattern of stress reaction in the body of the organism exposed to them. Thus, we define stressors by their consequences rather than by their own overt attributes. Common stressors are well-known, however. Prolonged fear, excessive heat or cold, fatigue, illness, and traumatic bodily injury are among the major stressors. Their effects, and those of other stressors produce a basic stress response in the body. This response can now be described in detail.

THE PITUITARY-ADRENAL AXIS

Among the more important changes in bodily function in stress are those that occur in the pituitary-adrenal axis (see Figure 5-1). When a particular stressor acts on the body, one consequence is that the pituitary gland releases from its anterior area a hormone known as *adrenocorticotrophic hormone* (ACTH). Once in the bloodstream, this hormone activates the adrenal glands. Activation of the adrenals leads to their secreting substances known as *corticoids* produced by the adrenal cortex. These corticoids are of two general types:

1. *Mineralocorticoids* or prophlogistic corticoids (P-Cs), stimulate the proliferative ability and reactivity of connective tissue. In effect, they improve the ability of the body to build barriers of connective tissue as a protection against further invasion by pathogens. Examples of these P-Cs are *deoxycorticosterone* (DOC) and *aldosterone.*
2. *Glucocorticoids* or *antiphlogistic corticoids* (A-Cs) are produced by the adrenal cortex, rather more generally and effectively, in fact, than P-Cs. The effect of A-Cs is to inhibit the development of connective tissue and thus reduce inflammation, but at the same time they make possible further invasion by pathogens.

Stress reactions involve, therefore, complex combinations of corticoids which have somewhat antagonistic functions in terms of the physical defenses of the body against pathogenic agents. It is beyond our scope here to discuss the physiological significance of these patterns,

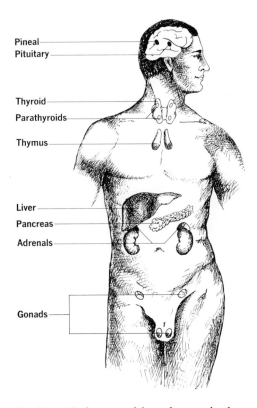

Pineal
Pituitary

Thyroid
Parathyroids

Thymus

Liver
Pancreas
Adrenals

Gonads

Fig. 5-1 *The location of the endocrine glands in the body, showing the position of the pituitary and the adrenals.*

but instead we should note that the presence of these corticoids makes available some crude measures of the extent of stress reactions in the individual patient. Circulating corticoids are metabolized into substances known as *corticosteroids,* and these, in some cases, are excreted in the urine. Urine samples may, therefore, be assayed to measure the changes in adrenal-pituitary activity via the increase in corticosteroids to be found in them. Two major members of the steroid substances are the *17-ketosteroids* and the *17-hydroxycorticosteroids* (17-OH-CS). These substances may be influenced by activities other than stress; the output of 17-ketosteroids is affected by the metabolism of *testosterone,* a hormone that is not an integral member of the stress response pattern.

Table 5.1   Principal Hormones and Their Major Functions

Gland	Hormone	Major functions
Anterior pituitary	Thyrotrophic (TTH)	Stimulates thyroid secretion
	Adrenocorticotrophic (ACTH)	Stimulates secretion of some hormones of adrenal cortex
	Lactogenic (prolactin)	Stimulates milk secretion by mammary glands
	Luteinizing (LH)	Development of interstitial cells of testis and ovary, and corpus luteum
	Follicle-stimulating (FSH)	Development of spermatogenic tissue in male and follicle in female
	Growth (STH)	Stimulates growth
Posterior pituitary	Oxytocin	Excites nonstriated muscles especially of uterus; excites mammary glands
	Vasopressin	Produces rise in blood pressure
	Antidiuretic	Prevents loss of water through kidney
Thyroid	Thyroxin	Influences metabolic rate
Parathyroid	Parathormone	Maintains calcium and phosphorous balance in blood
Islet cells	Insulin	Necessary for utilization of blood sugar

Table 5.1 Principal Hormones and Their Major Functions (cont.)

Gland	Hormone	Major functions
Adrenal cortex	Cortical steroids	Increased carbohydrate metabolism, sodium retention and potassium loss; some androgenic and estrogenic effects
Adrenal medulla	Epinephrine Norepinephrine	Increased sugar output by liver, stimulate most SNS end organs (differentially)
Ovary	Estrogen	Produces female primary and secondary sex characteristics
	Progesterone	Prepares uterus for implantation of embryo
Testis	Androgen (Testosterone)	Sexual arousal; produces primary and secondary sex characteristics

Source: Wenger, Jones, & Jones (1956), p. 230.

Nevertheless, their levels provide a crude but reasonable estimate of stress activity in the body. The functions of the various organs involved in hormone production are given in Table 5-1.

Temporal effects in stress. In the preceding paragraphs we have outlined the response of the pituitary-adrenal axis to brief stress. However, many patterns of psychopathology appear to be the outcome of prolonged exposure to stress, particularly to chronic fear. Thus, special importance has attached to the temporal effects of stress spread out over long periods of time. Although our knowledge is still sketchy, the general picture has been suggested by the work of Hans Selye (1957). Selye has described what he has called the *general adaptation syndrome*, referring to the sequence of adaptive responses and failures in the body under stress. Three stages are included in this sequence. In the first of these, the stage of *alarm*, the body responds by an increase in corticoid production irrespective of the site of any specific stressor (e.g., a local wound or burn). This is followed by the stage of *resistance,* in which defensive responses are localized at the point of stress. If this stage is prolonged, it will lead to the stage of *exhaustion,* at which point the local defenses break down and the general reaction takes over again. A schematic representation of this sequence is given in Figure 5-2.

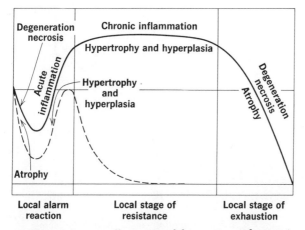

Fig. 5-2   *Schematic illustration of the sequence of events in the development of bodily response to stress. The three stages of alarm, resistance, and exhaustion are shown for both the local and general reaction systems. (Adapted from Selye, 1957)*

The stage of exhaustion involves the disintegration of the body's system of defenses against stress, and there is some significant possibility that pathology of other organs may develop at this point. Thus, prolonged stress may ultimately lead to malfunctioning of organs that have little direct biological relationship to the source of stress itself. We have already seen an example of this in our discussion of ulcers in Chapter 1. Here the stresses of army life produced changes in gastric secretion in some recruits, with the resulting ulcer formation. It is more than probable that, in the study concerned, there were other recruits who developed different kinds of psychosomatic disorder under that stress but were not detected by the investigators, because these disorders were not relevant to their investigation.

Adrenal ascorbic acid. When a state of stress exists, there is a depletion of ascorbic acid from the adrenals (where there is normally a store of it), and thus, the measurement of this depletion is a technique for the assay of the magnitude of the stress response. Assaying adrenal ascorbic

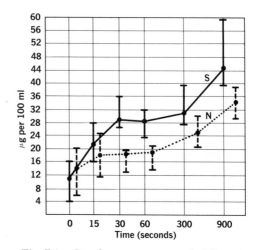

Fig. 5-3 *Circulating corticosteroids following an electric shock in rats that were stimulated in infancy (S) and rats that were not stimulated (N). The zero point on the abcissa represents values when no shock had been given, the solid circles are mean values, and the bars indicate the ranges of value around the means. (Levine, 1963)*

acid (AAA) involves the loss of the adrenals and hence of the experimental animal. For obvious reasons this technique can apply only to animal experimentation and then only when there is no requirement for behavioral measures taken after the stress condition has terminated.

Variables influencing the stress response. There are large individual differences in the extent to which a given stressor produces a pituitary-adrenal reaction. Some of these differences may be of genetic origin, but others may be due to differential early experience. Levine (1963) has reported that early exposure of animals to mild amounts of physical stress improves the later reactivity of the stress-resistance system, compared with that of animals given no early stress or given excessive early stress. Measurement of circulating corticosteroids provided one measure of these differences, and in Figure 5-3 we see the relative reactivity of a group given no stress in infancy compared with that of those given optimal stress.

It will be obvious that the study of stress resistance and its failure plays a large part in research into psychosomatic disorders. A history of long experience of stress of one kind (e.g., chronic anxiety) may well impair resistance to other stresses that may, in themselves, have no connection to the source of anxiety. Whatever this relationship between stress and psychosomatic disorder may be, its elucidation is one of the prime targets of contemporary psychopathologists.

The Autonomic Nervous System

The visceral organs of the body, including vascular and glandular structures, are supplied with nerves which activate them. These nerves, called *efferent* or *motor* nerves, collectively form the autonomic nervous system. Cell bodies of these nerves are generally located in ganglia that lie outside the spinal cord and are parallel to it. Thus the typical nerve leaves the spinal cord and synapses in a ganglion. At the ganglion, another neuron receives the impulse, carries it directly to the visceral organ, and activates the organ. The ganglia are located in several places. Two long chains running parallel and close to the spinal cord are known as the *sympathetic trunk*. Other ganglia are found in a *plexus* or network of nerve fibers, most of which are located in the abdominal cavity. A third group of ganglia are located directly near the organ to be activated. However, regardless of where the ganglion is located, the connection between the spinal cord and the viscera is always interrupted by one synapse, and this synapse occurs in a ganglion. Using this fact as a basis for description, we can identify a *preganglionic* fiber leading from the cord to the ganglion and a *postganglionic* fiber leading from the ganglion to the viscera. This is an important distinction, as will appear presently.

Ignoring certain complexities of anatomy, we may separate the autonomic system into (1) the craniosacral division and (2) the

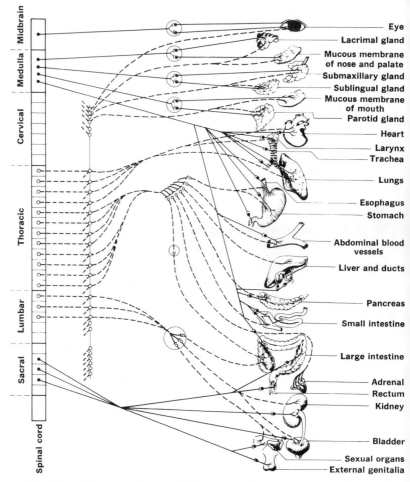

Fig. 5-4 *Schematic diagram of the autonomic nervous system, showing the supply of nerves to the viscera.*

thoracolumbar division. Craniosacral nerves emerge in the 3d, 7th, 9th, 10th, and 11th cranial nerves and in the 2d, 3d, and 4th sacral nerves. The thoracolumbar division includes nerves which emerge in the thoracic and upper lumbar nerves.

The thoracolumbar division has more commonly been called the *sympathetic* division, and the craniosacral division the *parasympathetic* division. Most visceral structures receive fibers from both the sympathetic and the parasympathetic system. Very often these two systems have antagonistic effects, as, for example, in the innervation of the iris of the eye. The iris has two sets of muscles, one which contracts the pupil and is activated by the parasympathetic system and the other which dilates the pupil and is controlled by sympathetic innervation. Thus, the continually changing size of the pupil is a result of the changing balance between the two kinds of nervous activity. A simplified diagram of the supply of autonomic nerves to the viscera is provided in Figure 5-4.

CHEMICAL PROPERTIES OF NERVE TRANSMISSION

From both preganglionic and postganglionic neurons, chemical substances are released when a nerve impulse reaches the end of the fiber. Generally speaking, all preganglionic fibers release a substance known as *acetylcholine.* Sympathetic postganglionic fibers release noradrenaline; parasympathetic postganglionic fibers release acetylcholine. This chemical difference does not correspond completely to the anatomical division between the craniosacral and thoracolumbar systems. For instance, the thoracolumbar supply to the human sweat glands is completely mediated by acetylcholine in both the preganglionic and postganglionic fibers. For general purposes of discussion, however, we can consider the basic functional divisions as being thoracolumbar-sympathetic-adrenergic on the one hand and craniosacral-parasympathetic-cholinergic on the other. Adrenergic and cholinergic refer to the role of adrenaline and acetylcholine respectively in activating the two kinds of fiber. Adrenaline and noradrenaline are also called epinephrine and norepinephrine.

THE ADRENAL MEDULLA

From the adrenal medulla, one of the endocrine glands, three substances are secreted: *adrenaline, noradrenaline,* and *dopamine.* These three substances are referred to as *catecholamines,* and we shall be mainly concerned with the first two. We have seen that, in addition to the production of catecholamines by the adrenal medulla, noradrena-line is produced by the sympathetic nerves. Both adrenaline and noradrenaline have also been found in urine and in blood. We can see that the sources and locations of these hormones are quite complex. We shall demonstrate shortly the differing effects they are believed to have upon emotional behavior.

Examination of the structure of the tissue of the adrenal medulla re-veals that it is composed of modified postganglionic sympathetic nerve cells. The catecholamines are stored in small particles in the cells and are released into the bloodstream when the splanchnic nerve leading to the adrenal medulla is stimulated. Activity of the splanchnic nerve is mediated by acetylcholine, and the same effect may be produced by giving a small injection of the substance methacholine or *Mecholyl* (acetyl-ß-methyl-choline). Immediately following this injection, there is an initial fall in blood pressure which is followed by a return to normal levels. However, there is a good deal of individual variability in this effect, and it has been developed by Funkenstein, Greenblatt, Rool, and Solomon (1949) as a method of testing the characteristic response of a subject's autonomic system.

THE MECHOLYL TEST

The standard procedure for the administration of Mecholyl is to inject a small quantity of the drug into the muscles of the arm and to record blood pressure and heart rate for about 15 to 20 minutes. Although there are marked differences in the manner in which subjects respond to this drug, Gellhorn has described three major types of reaction:

1. The blood pressure falls only slightly and briefly, returning to the base line after 3 to 5 minutes and then rising above the base line.

2. The blood pressure falls from 15 to 25 millimeters of mer-cury and then returns to the base line after about 5 to 8 minutes.

3. The blood pressure falls even more than in reaction 2 above and does not return to the base line within 15 minutes (Gell-horn & Loofbourrow, 1963).

With increasing age, there is a tendency for people to move from the first to the third type of reaction, i.e., to show less sympathetic activity after the Mecholyl has been injected. The significance of the Mecholyl test in relation to particular patterns of behavior disorder will be discussed later.

THE CATECHOLAMINES AND EMOTION

Several lines of research have suggested that the effects of adrenaline and noradrenaline may be related to the experiences of anxiety and anger respectively. When a subject is given adrenaline and then Mecholyl, there is a large fall in blood pressure, as in Gellhorn's reaction 3. However, if the subject has received noradrenaline before the Mecholyl, then there is only a slight fall in blood pressure. From this observation it might be argued that the response of a normal subject to the Mecholyl test will indicate whether there is an adrenaline or a noradrenaline dominance in the typical response of his adrenal medulla. Pursuing this line of reasoning, Funkenstein, King, and Drolette (1953) report that young men faced with a stress situation responded by overt anger, self-blame for their inadequacy, or simple anxiety. Those who exhibited open anger (Funkenstein referred to this as "anger-out") showed a noradrenaline pattern to Mecholyl injection, whereas those who revealed self-blame ("anger-in") or anxiety revealed an adrenaline pattern of reaction on the Mecholyl test.

A very similar line of evidence comes from an investigation by Ax (1953) in which he led subjects to believe that they might receive an electric shock from defective wiring of a circuit. Those who reacted with anger produced a noradrenaline reaction, and those who responded with fear showed an adrenaline reaction. These data suggest that there are hormonal differences between the two states of emotion —anger and fear; they also suggest that there are individual differences in the typical hormonal reaction to threat and, therefore, in the accompanying emotion. Experiments that have attempted to demonstrate the reverse proposition—that injections of one or the other of the catecholamines can generate the appropriate emotional experience— have not been reliably successful, unless the experimenter provided external cues to what the desired emotion should be (Schacter & Singer, 1962). Emotional experiences must be regarded as the correlates of very complicated patterns of bodily activity, invoking mechanisms that are much more subtle than simple hormonal processes.

We have already seen that the activities of the sympathetic and the parasympathetic divisions of the autonomic nervous system are generally antagonistic. In anger or fear, the predominant activity is sympathetic and is mediated by adrenaline or noradrenaline. Ignoring the specific differences in the effects of these catecholamines, we may

Table 5.2 *Parasympathetic and Sympathetic Nervous System Functions*

Organ	Response	Sympathetic effect	Parasympathetic effect
Heart	Rate	Increases	Lowers
Lungs	Dilate	Facilitates	Inhibits
Blood vessels at periphery	Constriction	Facilitates	Inhibits
Sweat glands	Secrete	Facilitates	Inhibits
Eyes	Iris	Dilates	Contracts
Lachrymal glands	Weeping	Inhibits	Facilitates
Salivary glands	Salivation	Inhibits	Facilitates
Gastrointestinal tract	Peristalsis	Inhibits	Facilitates
Glands in stomach	Secretion of acid, pepsin, and mucus	Inhibits	Facilitates

briefly review the general bodily changes that occur with sympathetic activity. These are summarized in Table 5-2. Also provided in the table are the related and often antagonistic functions served by the parasympathetic division of the autonomic nervous system.

POLYGRAPHIC MEASUREMENT

Direct assay of hormonal or nervous system activity is not readily feasible in the intact normal subject. Even when it is possible to take blood specimens, the procedures involved in taking them are likely to produce some emotional reaction. Furthermore, the time that must elapse between taking such a sample and completing its analysis is an obstacle to the continuous observation of bodily states during different kinds of external stimulation. Because of this, research investigators have for many years used an indirect measure of different aspects of bodily activity, namely, the polygraphic recording of the electrical side effects produced by this bodily activity.

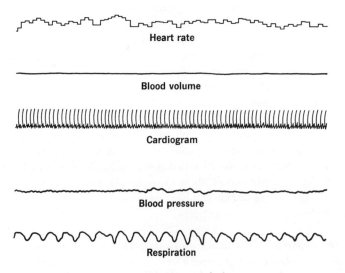

Heart rate

Blood volume

Cardiogram

Blood pressure

Respiration

Fig. 5-5 *Example of polygraph record showing various measures of cardiac activity and rate of respiration.*

The polygraph consists of a series of devices that are responsive to the movement of various parts of the body or that detect electrical changes accompanying the movements. Each of these devices relays the signals of the changing activity that are first amplified considerably and then used to deflect a pen across a moving paper chart. An example is shown in Figure 5-5. Typical measures taken and their normal characteristics are as follows.

The electrocardiogram (EKG). As the heart beats, the muscular contractions involved produce a certain standard sequence of electrical activity that may be detected by placing electrodes on the body surface near the heart. The distance from one peak to another on the record represents one beat of the heart, and the rate at which the individual's heart is beating may, in turn, be recorded as an additional but separate aspect of the activity of the heart. The latter measure is recorded by a *cardiotachometer;* it can also be computed by simply measuring the time between each beat on the electrocardiogram directly.

The electromyogram (EMG). Activation of a muscle produces electrical changes that may also be recorded in a manner much the same as that used in the EKG. Unlike the EKG, however, the frequency or rate of the wave produced by muscular activity is quite variable and can reach very high frequencies. A typical EMG record demonstrates periodic bursts of activity when a muscle is activated and low-frequency changes when a muscle is relatively relaxed.

The plethysmogram. The volume of blood at the periphery of the body changes with autonomic activity, as we have already seen. Blood volume measures are also recorded polygraphically with a plethysmograph. As we might expect, these changes take place slowly compared with the changes in muscle and heart potential, and the typical record is one of slow, irregular fluctuations.

The galvanic skin response and skin potential. With fear, there is increased activity of the sweat glands located near the surface of the body. When an electrode is placed on the body and put in circuit with a galvanometer, any change in the resistance at the electrode will produce a deflection of the galvanometer. Sweating will reduce resistance on skin surfaces, and thus, if we place the electrode on the palm of the hand, we are likely to get a fairly responsive measure of palmar perspiration by recording these changes in resistance. This kind of response has been called the galvanic skin response and the *psychogalvanic reflex* (PGR). Alternatively, we may measure the potential difference between two points on the body—this measure being called *galvanic skin potential* (GSP).

Blood pressure. Our earlier discussion of the Mecholyl test indicated the usefulness of measurement of blood pressure changes in studying autonomic functions. Blood pressure is typically measured with an instrument called a *sphygmomanometer,* and here again we may maintain a continuous record of changes in pressure by polygraphic means.

There are several problems connected with the use of the polygraph. One set of problems is essentially mechanical. Variations in the electrical properties of the electrodes attached to the subject, artifact produced by the interference of one system in the recording of another (for

Table 5.3   Intercorrelations Among Various Autonomic Measures, Age, Reaction Time, Premorbid History, and Drug Dosage in a Group of Schizophrenic Patients (Crider, et al., 1965, p. 204)

	Premorbid adjustment	Reaction time	Skin potential level	Heart rate	Age
Reaction time	.62°				
Skin potential level	.62°	.54†			
Heart rate	.21	.29	.52†		
Age	−.32	−.12	−.20	−.44	
Drug dosage	.02	−.15	−.13	.12	−.17

° $p < .01$, two-tailed.
† $p < .03$, two-tailed.

example, respiration tends to affect heart rate recording), actual unreliability in the components of the polygraphic amplifying system, and the like, may all act to produce error in the final record. The solutions to these problems are largely matters of apparatus construction and proper training of the operator to recognize and prevent them.

Another set of problems has to do with the reliability of the measures. To the extent that we hope to use the magnitude of an autonomic response as a variable in a study of emotional behavior in schizophrenia, for example, it is necessary to be sure that the response will be the same from day to day when measured under similar conditions. If it varies widely from day to day, then we have low test-retest reliability (See Chapter 1, page 19). There has been conflicting evidence on this point.

Lacey, Bateman, and Van Lehn (1953) report relatively high reliability of autonomic measures, but Kaelbling, King, Achenbach, Branson, and Pasamanick (1960) found it to be low. The status of the question is still far from clear.

For an example of one of the many studies of autonomic functioning in psychopathology, we can turn to Crider, Grinspoon, and Maher (1965). These investigators studied 20 male schizophrenic patients varying in their length of stay in hospital and in the adequacy of their premorbid history of social adjustment. Subjects were then placed in an experimental situation requiring them to react rapidly to an auditory stimulus. Speed of reaction time was correlated with polygraphic measures of heart rate and skin potential. The further correlations with premorbid adjustment, age, and dosages of therapeutic drugs received were also computed. The data obtained are given in Table 5-3. From these correlations we see that premorbid adjustment, reaction time, and GSP form a cluster of mutually significant correlations but that the other measures are unrelated.

TELEMETRY

Conventional methods of polygraphic measurement involve attaching wires between the subject and a rather heavy, static recording system. Consequently, it is limited to use under conditions in which the subject may be studied in a permanent laboratory. When the technique has been used in the study of stress, it has been necessary to create stresses in the laboratory—a tactic that runs the risk of producing rather artificial kinds of stress, or stresses of rather lower intensity than occur in the natural habitat. In recent years, however, a partial solution to this problem has been found in the use of a radio link between the subject and the apparatus, replacing the conventional direct wire link. This technique, known as *radiotelemetry* or, more usually, *telemetry,* depends upon the placing of a miniature radio transmitter directly on the subject. The battery-powered transmitter has a limited range of transmission that does not often exceed 200 or 300 yards. Typical signals (EKG, EMG) are received by a radio receiver, amplified, and then recorded on a chart or oscilloscope in much the same way that we see with the conventional polygraph. Provided that the receiving station can be set up within the requisite range, it is then possible to monitor autonomic responses in the natural habitat. This greatly increases the variety of real stresses that can be studied. Figure 5-6 depicts the attachment of a radiotelemetry transmitter to a human subject.

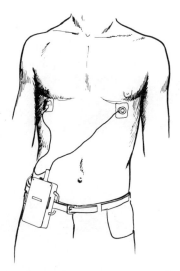

Fig. 5-6 *Radio telemetry transmitter attached to human subject for transmission of EKG.*

The use of this system by psychologists is relatively new, and there has not yet developed a body of literature pertaining to it. However, preliminary reports (e.g., Liebner, 1966) suggest that the magnitudes of autonomic response obtained in the natural habitat are much greater than those obtained with laboratory stresses. She compared rates obtained from student subjects during final examinations with those obtained in the laboratory while they were doing mental arithmetic and speeded word association tasks. These latter are common laboratory "stresses," but her data indicated that heart rates during the examinations were much higher than those recorded in the laboratory and that correlations between an individual's heart rate in the laboratory and that during the final examination were nonsignificant. Although these data can be regarded only as suggestive, they raise a rather important question of the validity of laboratory measures of stress response as indicators of stress response in the natural habitat. With increased use of telemetry, we may expect to find answers to this question.

An additional insight into the balance of the divisions of the autonomic nervous system may be obtained by studying the rate at which the pupil of the eye dilates and contracts under appropriate stimulation. When the intensity of illumination falling on the eye is increased, the pupil

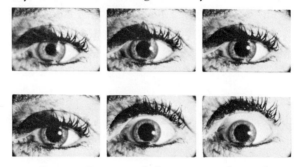

Fig. 5-7 *Sequence of changes in pupil size of the human eye as it dilates under light stimulation.* (*Photograph courtesy Mildred Dubitzky*)

contracts—a response mediated largely by cholinergic activity. Reduction of light intensity results in pupillary dilation—an adrenergic response. By using controlled light intensities, it is possible to photograph the size of the pupil at different time intervals during either dilation or contraction and thus to plot the rate at which these responses are occurring. From these data, individuals may then be compared with the norm for their age as to the rate of response. Overactivity or underactivity of the two divisions of the system may be identified and used as a basis for diagnosing pathology in one or both of them. Figure 5-7 shows typical pupil films obtained with this technique.

This technique has been used in two ways. The rate of dilation or contraction may be used as an estimate of the functioning of the adrenergic and cholinergic systems and thus provide a general measure of autonomic system activity. Alternatively, alterations in pupil size may be used to infer motivational states in subjects, pupil dilation representing an index of motivational arousal.

An example of the first use is to be found in an experiment by Fowles (1966). He studied the rates of pupillary contraction and dilation in schizophrenic and normal subjects, as well as heart rate, skin potential, and performance on psychomotor tasks. He found that final pupil size did discriminate between schizophrenic patients with a good premorbid history and those with a poor history. The latter had smaller final pupil sizes either dilated or constricted than did the former.

The use of pupillary responses to measure motivation is seen in a paper by Hess, Seltzer, and Shlien (1965). They studied the pupil response of two groups of young male subjects. One group was known to have homosexual interests and activities, the other was known to be exclusively heterosexual in interest. Pupil response was measured to slides of quasi-nude or nude pictures of females and males. The form of their data are given in Figure 5-8. As the figure shows, pupil dilation significantly differentiated the two groups of subjects in this experiment. Pupil size cannot readily be controlled voluntarily and hence offers interesting possibilities as a nonfakeable valid measure of motivational arousal. There are, however, many technical problems in obtaining reliable measurements, and this technique must still be regarded as in a proving stage.

ELECTROENCEPHALOGRAPHY

When electrodes are attached to the scalp of a human subject, it is possible to record current of fluctuating voltage. When this is amplified and connected to a chart and penwriter, the current produces movements of the pen that appear as waves on the moving chart. The discovery of this phenomenon is credited to Hans Berger in 1924,[2] and the wave discovered was referred to as the Berger rhythm. Since that time, the development of methods of detecting and recording electrical rhythms in the brain has proceeded rapidly; the technique is termed *electroencephalography* (EEG).

Although the use of surface electrodes is standard practice in clinical electroencephalography, research investigators may from time to time use electrodes that are directly in contact with nervous tissue. Direct placement of electrodes in the brain or the brainstem is not uncommon when animals are being studied, and it is also used in some instances

[2] Schwab (1951) reports that these waves had been observed in 1918 by a medical student at Harvard but had been ignored at that time.

when human patients are undergoing brain surgery. Characteristic wave patterns are found, depending upon the placement and type of the electrode. Various forms of brain pathology also produce deviant rhythms, and these may be used as an aid to diagnosis in clinical neurol-

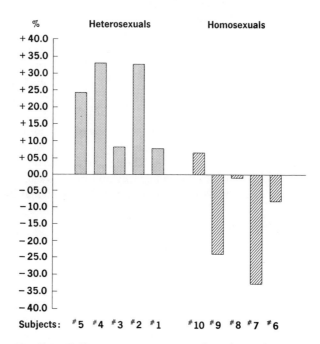

Fig. 5-8 *Differences in percentage of pupil-size change in response to male and female pictures. (A positive score shows higher response to pictures of females; a negative score shows higher response to pictures of males.) (Hess, Seltzer, & Shilien, 1965)*

ogy. The broad group of brain dysfunctions that is termed "epilepsy" is of particular interest in clinical EEG, since the dysfunctions are associated with a tendency to produce certain kinds of atypical waves.

In normal subjects, the two main frequencies found are the *alpha* rhythm and the *beta* rhythm. Alpha waves are of a frequency between 8 and 13 cycles per second (cps), and beta waves are in the range of 14 to 25 cps. Other frequencies sometimes identified are *delta* (0.5 to 3.5 cps),

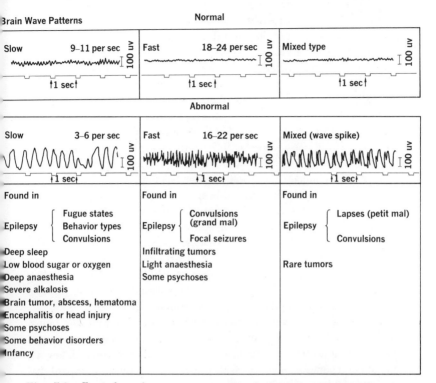

Fig. 5-9 *Examples of common normal and deviant EEG rhythmns.* (*Schwab, 1951*)

theta (4 to 7 cps), and *gamma* (26 cps and higher). Alpha rhythms are ordinarily found when electrodes are placed in the occipital and parietal areas, and beta frequency is found in the frontal and central areas. Alpha frequency is readily blocked or eliminated by certain kinds of external stimulation, especially visual stimulation. It may also be blocked by certain kinds of conscious activity, but the conditions under which this blocking occurs are not as yet clearly established. Examples of these rhythms are given in Figure 5-9.

EEG and psychopathology. There have been many investigations of the relationship between EEG deviations and behavioral deviations. In their broadest sense, these investigations have been undertaken because of an implicit hypothesis that much pathological behavior is determined by some dysfunction of the central nervous system. However, the precise relationship of an EEG deviation to a particular kind of organic pathology is often unclear, and consequently the hypothesis rarely gets beyond a statement that patients with deviant behavior might be expected to show some (unspecified) aberration on their EEG tracing.

This kind of research suffers from several intrinsic weaknesses. The sheer lack of specificity means that there is an increased chance of finding EEG deviations and hence, incorrectly, accepting the hypothesis as valid. When the investigator commits himself to looking for a particular type of EEG anomaly, the results may be less impressive.

Psychotic patients in a mental hospital tend, on the whole, to come from the lower socioeconomic strata of a community. Poorer physical health is more commonly found in the same population, and we should expect to find a higher incidence of almost any kind of bodily disorder than we find in a comparable group of people from higher economic levels. A sheer count of the number of EEG anomalies (including epilepsies) in a mental hospital population should, therefore, reveal a higher frequency than that found in the community at large.

Drugs affect the type of EEG trace to be found in a human being. With the increasing use of tranquilizing drugs in hospital populations, a further complication is introduced into this kind of research. Likewise, metabolic changes associated with prolonged exposure to hospital diet and general hospital environment may interfere with a straightforward interpretation of brain rhythms.

Bearing these factors in mind, we find that the data from *clinical* EEG are as yet of little use in diagnosing psychopathology. Hill (1950) has commented, "At present the practical value of electroencephalography for the psychiatrist is to enable him to know more about the organic cerebral disorder and little else [p. 363]." Although this statement is still true for the data obtained from conventional electroencephalography, there have been developments in the recording of electrical activity in the brain that promise more sophisticated insights into psychopathology. One of these techniques involves the evoking of electrical activity in the cortex by stimulation of a sensory nerve. Input generated by this stimulation produces momentary electrical excitation in the relevant sensory cortex. However, the amount of excitation is so small, compared with the normal fluctuations of the EEG, that it is extremely difficult to detect by simple visual inspection of the EEG tracing. However, it can be detected cumulatively by superimposing many segments of EEG tracing on top of one another so that the minute additional excitation in any one instance is multiplied by its occurrence in many instances. Shagass and Schwartz (1962) report the use of this technique to detect the excitability of the nervous systems in a variety of psychopathological groups.

Excitability is defined here in terms of the speed and magnitude of a cortical response to external stimulation. Also measured is the length of time it takes for the cortical activity to return to normal. Various measures of this recovery process indicated that it was attentuated in schizophrenia, psychotic depression, and a miscellany of personality disorders but was faster than normal in patients with neurotic depression and anxiety. The possibility that behavior disorders may be related to the relative cortical balance between inhibition and excitation has already been described in Chapter 2 (see p. 48) with reference to the work of Eysenck. It is to this work that Shagass and Schwartz referred in interpreting their results—providing us with a neat example of the connection between a biological-behavioral theory and work in the EEG laboratory.

Brain pathology and EEG. Any deviant form may be a basis for suspecting the presence of brain pathology in the subject. Certain kinds of cerebral malfunction are correlated with certain specific EEG phenomena, but the organic pathology often produces abnormal EEG trackings of a nonspecific kind. Equally important is the fact that deviant or atypical EEG patterns are found in a percentage of the normal population. Thus, the diagnosis of brain pathology from EEG alone is a rather uncertain procedure subject to some perceptible margin of error.

We have already mentioned the emphasis placed on EEG in the diagnosis of epilepsy. To complete our discussion of this topic, let us mention the better-known varieties of EEG abnormalcy. There are many possible variations of the normal rhythms of the EEG. Classification systems are not completely standardized either, but one of the more widely used is that developed at the Harvard Medical School by Gibbs, Gibbs, and Lennox (1943), sometimes called the "Harvard group." Four major categories of frequencies are used in this classification:

1. *Paroxysmal.* This includes five categories of pattern found in conjunction with epileptic seizures:
    a. Petit mal
    b. Petit mal variant
    c. Grand mal
    d. Spikes
    e. Psychomotor
2. *Normal.* Frequencies in the alpha and beta wave bands
3. *Slow.*
    S.1.   Theta activity
    S.2.   Delta activity
4. *Fast.*
    F.1.   Activity of 14 to 20 cps
    F.2.   Activity of higher frequency than beta

Among the paroxysmal group, all but the spike frequency are named for their association with particular clinical types of epileptic seizure. Spike frequencies are seen in many kinds of epileptic record but are also found in a variety of other anomalies. Like the slow- and fast-activity groups, the spike is generally regarded as evidence of some dysfunction but is not specific to any one kind of pathology or to any one kind of behavioral manifestation. These frequencies are illustrated in Figure 5-9 above.

Arousal and Activation

When a stimulus impinges upon an individual, it has two kinds of effect. One of these is the *arousal* or *activation* of the subject, the other is the guiding or selective effect the stimulus has upon the response made to it. The guiding effect is contingent, to a large extent, upon past learning in relation to the stimulus. On the other hand, the more general effect of arousal is common to all stimuli and represents a nonspecific consequence of stimulation per se.

All states of activity of an organism might be graded along a dimension from complete rest to maximum arousal. Deep sleep would thus constitute the lowest end of the arousal continuum, and the more aroused states would progress through light sleep up to wakefulness and then through various stages of tension and excitement. Arousal, as we are using it here, refers to a biological state of a living organism. Although there are many correlations among the physiological measures of arousal and overt measures of behavior, these are not perfect. Consequently, we must emphasize that arousal is a *state* of the organism and that the state of arousal is not always directly reflected in overt behavior. It is quite possible for a person to be highly aroused but inactive from the viewpoint of an observer.

MEASURES OF AROUSAL

Different investigators have tended to emphasize different measures of arousal. However, there is general acceptance of three measures:

1. *Desynchronization of the EEG.* When a stimulus occurs while a subject is producing alpha frequency in the EEG record, this frequency is blocked and gives way to beta waves. These beta waves are considerably less synchronized than the alpha frequency, i.e., they do not have the same regularity and smoothness that we find in alpha. For one group of investigators this *desynchronization* is a standard measure of arousal (e.g., Lindsley, 1959).

2. *Palmar conductance.* Measures of the electrical conductance of the surface of the palm of the hand indicate the amount of activity of sweat glands in that area. Palmar conductance is thus one of the measures related to similar techniques for recording skin resistance and skin potential.

3. *Muscle tension.* Muscular tension has also been used as a measure of arousal, the recording being made in the manner described previously in the section on polygraphy.

Although these three measures have been the major ones employed, the use of other signs of autonomic activity (e.g., heart rate) has been reported from time to time. It will be apparent that the measures used to define arousal overlap considerably with those used to define responses to stress. Indeed, the introduction of the concept of arousal would have nothing to offer the psychologist if it were simply another term to describe the pattern of bodily responses to external stimulation. Of much greater interest, however, is the relationship demonstrated between measures of arousal and measures of behavior.

When talking about the relationship between stimulation and responses, we have confined ourselves so far to discussions of the effects of learning. Motivation has been discussed in terms of specific drives or needs attributable to internal or external stimulation and in determining the kinds of stimuli that will be attended to in the environment. With the concept of arousal, we turn to consider the relationship between responses and a general state of the organism. In the sleeping state we find that measures of arousal and measures of organized overt behavior are both low. When we begin to increase the level of arousal of an organism, we find an increase in the efficiency of its behavior. "Efficiency" is not a simple question of the intensity of a response or the amount of sheer activity we find in the subject. If we require a subject to respond as quickly as possible to the appearance of a light by pressing a button, the speed with which this is done is a measure of efficiency. If we require a complicated discrimination among many different kinds of lights, and speed of response is not essential, then the lack of error is our measure of efficiency. "Level of performance" is often used in lieu of "efficiency" as a descriptive term, and for our purposes here the two are interchangeable.

One of the simplest and clearest illustrations of the relationship between arousal and level of performance is provided in a study described by Malmo (1959), already mentioned in Chapter 3. Since the experimental logic of this relationship is important in understanding the arousal concept, we shall describe it here. Rats deprived of water were measured for heart rate at different degrees of deprivation. The results were quite straightforward: as the amount of thirst increased, the heart rate of the animals increased. Using heart rate as a measure of arousal, the experimenters thus established the connection between the arousing condition (thirst) and a physiological measure of the arousal state (heart rate). Meantime, the animals were placed in an operant chamber and received water by depressing a bar in the chamber—a standard operant situation. With increasing thirst, the rate of bar pressing went up, as we should naturally expect. This increase was observed for up to 48 hours of deprivation, but at higher levels of thirst, the rate began to drop again. Thus, although heart rate showed maximum arousal, response rate showed a decline. Figure 5-10 shows this relationship graphically.

In an experiment of this kind, there is the obvious possibility that high levels of thirst produce physical weakness in the animal and that this accounts for the decline in response rate. Control for this problem

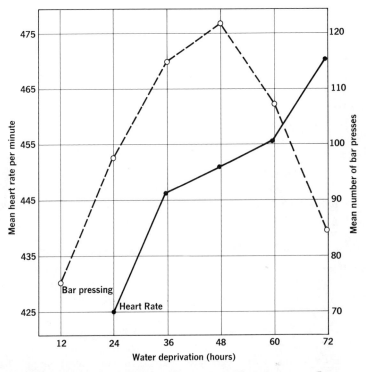

Fig. 5-10 *The inverted U-curve of arousal and performance. Depriva-tion of water increases both arousal (as measured by heart rate) and per-formance in a bar-pressing task. After 48 hours, arousal continues to in-crease, but performance begins to be impaired. (Belanger & Feldman, cited by Malmo, 1958)*

was provided by spacing each deprivation session between several days of ad lib. drinking. Further, the experimenters noted that there was lit-tle difference in weight across the various degrees of thirst.

The relationship among degree of stimulation, extent of arousal, and level of performance shown in Figure 5-10 is central to the concept of arousal as it relates to behavior. Workers in this field refer to it as an inverted U curve, and it appears in many experiments and under many different conditions.

When we consider the importance of attentional focusing—the "tuning out" of irrelevant stimulation—for normal integrated behavior, we can appreciate the disorganization that would arise if the tuning-out process was defective. All kinds of unwanted stimulation would enter consciousness and interfere with proper concentration on the main stimuli of interest at the time. We can get some rudimentary idea of what this would be like when we play back a home tape recording we have made ourselves. If the recording was of a friend speaking, for example, we may be astonished to hear the sound of automobile horns, traffic noises, passing airplanes, distant coughs. These were all recorded faithfully as they happened but at a time when we were attending only to the material meant to be recorded, and we did not notice the presence of all this other sound input. Now, on the tape, they are disruptive.

Presumably, something like this would happen in the conscious experience of a patient who has defective attentional focusing. Since we have already seen that good focusing of attention is associated with heightened levels of arousal, we might hypothesize that this "tape recorder" experience would be found in people with pathologically low levels of arousal. Additionally, we might expect that anything that could raise arousal levels in such people would improve their attentional focusing and lead to more effective responding. The converse would also be true.

Agnew and Agnew (1963), for example, using normal subjects studied the effect of increased arousal, produced by threat of shock and evidenced by increased heart rate, upon narrowness of attention in a perceptual task. The predicted narrowing was found.

Crider et al. (1965) repeated an experiment of Tizard and Venables (1957), confirming the original finding that the attention of schizophrenic patients is improved, as shown by their faster response on a reaction-time task, when the experimenter increases arousal with the addition of extraneous white noise during the task. White noise increases arousal by virtue of its general quality as sensory input. Without this additional arousal condition, schizophrenic patients were significantly slower and more erratic in their reaction-time values than normal controls. The effect of arousal was to bring their performance up to levels indistinguishable from that of normal controls under normal conditions. Hence, it seems plausible to conclude that the ordinarily poor performance of the schizophrenic is attributable to a pathologically low level of arousal in normal environmental circumstances.

Returning to the findings of Shagass and Schwartz (1962) cited previously, we see that some pathological conditions seem to be marked by excessively high excitability, and hence, probably by high levels of arousal. Anxiety state and neurotic depression were the two conditions mentioned in their data in which this appeared to be the case. Thus, deficiencies of arousal may well be reflected in too little or too much arousal. Since the biological mechanisms controlling the arousal state of an individual are extremely complex, it is apparent that many possibilities for biological pathology exist. Such pathologies could produce either overarousal or underarousal. A clear understanding of the role of arousal systems in various psychopathologies is clearly a distant goal.

We should also note that experiments in which direct measures of central nervous system states are not made are simply inferential rather than demonstrative of a biological process. The Tizard and Venables study did not measure any biological variable directly. Attentional narrowing was *inferred* from improved reaction times: arousal was *assumed* to have been increased by extraneous sensory input. The Shagass and Schwartz (1962) study, on the other hand, did measure a central nervous system state more directly and hence produced results that have less possibility of ambiguous interpretation.

CENTRAL AROUSAL MECHANISMS

When diverse stimuli have some effects in common, we are not surprised to find that they are "processed" by some common system within the organism. The very observation of the nonspecific arousing properties of so many different kinds of events leads us to look for some unitary structure or system which is affected the same way by all stimuli. Evidence now available suggests that the most likely candidate for this role is a complex group of structures within the central nervous system known collectively as the *reticular activating system* (RAS). This system may be divided into two functional parts, one of which is called the *ascending* reticular activating system (ARAS). Stimuli received by the sense receptors of the subject not only are channeled to the appropriate sensory area of the brain but also have an additional route to the ARAS. Although the structure of the ARAS is extremely complex, the main structures are the reticular formation of the medial brainstem and parts

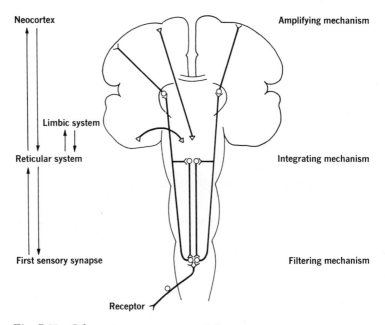

Fig. 5-11 *Schematic representation of the main neuronal circuits comprising the reticular activating system.* (*From Hernandez-Péon, 1961*)

of the hypothalamus and thalamus. Once received by this system, impulses are directed widely to all parts of the cortex. When they are received by the cortex, their function seems to be not to provide information about the specific stimulus which initiated the arousal (that information is discriminated at the primary sensory area) but, more simply, to keep the cortex active.

The second division of the reticular activating system is the descending system. Descending fibers in this system appear to inhibit incoming sensory impulses or prevent them from getting to the sensory areas of the cortex. Several electrophysiologists have repeatedly demonstrated that, in a condition of arousal produced by an external stimulus, sensory impulses from other kinds of stimulation are prevented from reaching the cortex. Loosely speaking, we might state that the effect of the descending components of the reticular system is to "damp down" other stimuli and thus facilitate selective attention to the initial arousal stimulus.

A schematic version of the operation of the reticular activating system is given in Figure 5-11.

Summary

We can see from these discussions that biological research into behavior pathology is still relatively crude. Measurements taken with EEG, the polygraph, pupillography, etc., are gross and physically superficial. We do not yet know the way in which many different variables affect single measures of these kinds. However, it has been found fruitful to organize these gross observations around the concepts of stress and arousal. It is clear that biological contributions to psychopathology are often of a fundamental nature and that a proper knowledge of them is an essential part of the equipment of the psychopathologist.

CHAPTER 6

GENETIC AND EPIDEMIOLOGIC
METHODS

Psychopathologists have long been interested in two broad classes of phenomenon that they meet in their investigations. One of these is the fact that certain societies or social classes have fewer, or more, instances of some pathologies than other societies do. This would suggest, at first sight, that there are environmental influences operating on these groups that are either unusually malignant in producing psychopathology or unusually beneficial in preventing it. Investigations of this phenomenon have drawn on the concepts and techniques of anthropology, sociology, and *epidemiology* (the study of the distribution of a disorder in various populations). We shall discuss these concepts in this chapter.

The second phenomenon is the fact that people exposed to the same environment do not always (or even frequently) develop the psychopathology that others in that environment do. Schofield and Balian (1959), for example, examined the personal histories of 178 schizophrenic patients and 150 normals. The latter were individuals drawn from the same social class as the schizophrenics and were patients receiving treatment for physical illness. Many comparisons were made between these groups on variables relating to relations with parents, siblings, school adjustment, school achievement, and the like. The most striking finding of this study was that many of the childhood influences thought to be pathogenic for schizophrenia were found in sizable percentages among the normal controls. So-called traumatic histories were found in nearly one-fourth of the normal controls, while relationships characterized as ambivalent, indifferent, or hostile were slightly *more* frequent between the parents of the normals than between the parents of the schizophrenics!

This latter kind of observation suggests that there may be an inborn vulnerability to psychopathology. Thus, the study of the inheritance of behavior disorders has become a prime area of investigation, and a serious understanding of abnormal behavior now requires a working knowledge of the concepts and findings of genetics. We shall now turn to these for more detailed examination.

Basic Genetic Principles

Among the contents of the nucleus of the living cell is a material known as *chromatin*. At times of cell division, this material becomes more or-

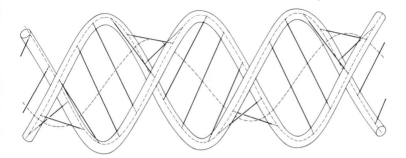

Fig. 6-1 *Model of DNA structure is a double helix with slanted cross-links connecting the two chains. The nucleic acid chains which form the helixes are identical but head in opposite directions. The cross-links (solid straight lines) consist of complementary pairs of side chains connected by hydrogen bonds. A broken line traces the centers of the cross-links and also forms a helix. (Crick, 1957; courtesy Scientific American, Inc.)*

ganized and appears as a series of paired structures known as *chromosomes*. This number of pairs is 23 in man and is known as the *diploid number*. Twenty-two of these pairs are known as *autosomal chromosomes*, and the 23d pair determines the sex of the individual. During cell division by the process of *mitosis*, a single cell divides into two "daughter" cells, each of which gets one member of each pair of chromosomes, and thus the two cells are identical in their chromosomal composition.

During sexual mating and the accompanying process of cell division called *meiosis*, the cell divides in such a fashion that the resulting cells each have one-half of the total chromosomes. Since the process determining which half of all the pairs goes into any one cell is apparently random, there are 23^2 possible chromosome patterns available. The new cell, called the *gamete*, unites with a gamete from the other parent to form a new single cell with the total chromosomes restored to the full number of 23 pairs. The number of possible genetic combinations from any one pair of parents is thus somewhat in excess of 8 million.

At present, there appears to be little doubt that the basic genetic material is *deoxyribonucleic acid* (DNA). This is a compound of large molecular weight containing a number of nucleotides joined together in a long, spiral chain. Two such chains intertwine to form a double helix (see Figure 6-1).

During cell division, it seems likely that the two chains of the helix separate and that each one then provides a pattern for the synthesis of the other so that the complementary chain is formed and the double helix reconstructed in each of the new cells. We also know that DNA chain sequences may be affected by radiation and that other disruptions of the sequence of the chains can occur. These disruptions are likely to be transmitted to subsequent cells produced by cell division and to have possible effects upon the development or behavior of the organism.

The chromosomes may be seen with the aid of the microscope. Photographs taken of the chromosomes permit us to identify the pairs by arranging them according to size. Such a photograph is known as a *karyotype,* an example of which is shown in Figure 6-2. Karyotyping enables us to recognize deviant pairings of the chromosomes, and this kind of deviancy has been found to be significant in the genesis of some kinds of psychopathology (e.g., the investigations of Down's syndrome reported by Lejeune, Turpin, & Gautier, 1959). Although chromosomal aberrations may account for some kinds of behavioral and developmental defect, the main burden of research is directed at a level of analysis of a considerably finer kind, namely, the detection of deviation related to the influence of *genes.*

The gene is the simplest unit of heredity. We do not yet know that such a unit exists in the sense that there is a physical unit discriminably different from others and occupying some location on the chromosome. For the present, the gene must be thought of as a hypothetical entity whose existence is postulated to account for empirical findings in studies of heredity. In this hypothetical status the gene is regarded as a unit lying on a *locus* of the chromosome. The number of genes involved in the 23 human chromosomes has been variously estimated at between 2,000 and 50,000 (Stern, 1960). Genes produce their action via a series of biological steps involving the agency of various proteins and enzymes. These catalyze (or inhibit) various biochemical reactions in the cell which, in turn, influence biological and physiological systems at a grosser level. In many cases, the final biological outcome may not have any notable effect upon behavior, as in the genetic determination of eye color. In other cases the gene may have no effect upon overt biological processes unless the action of the gene is itself facilitated by some special circumstances.

A given genetic pattern at the biochemical level may produce an ul-

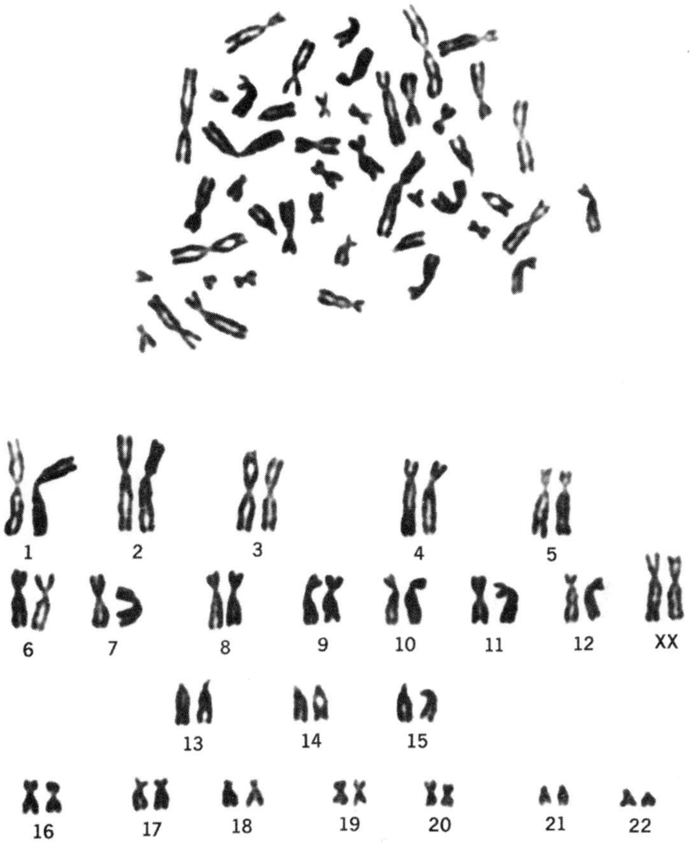

Fig. 6-2 *Karyotype of normal human female, showing chromosomes arranged and numbered according to size in the lower half of the photograph. (Photograph courtesy of Prof. W. M. Davidson, London)*

timate behavioral pattern that includes several behavioral variations, the specific variation observed in any one case being the result of nongenetic factors mainly of an environmental kind. The behavioral manifestations are referred to, generally, as the *phenotype*, while the underlying genetic pattern is known as the *genotype*. We should notice that the patterns of behavior that strike a psychologist as interesting or significant may not in any way reflect the existence of an underlying genotype. By the same token, the discovery of the phenotypical pattern produced by a genotype may not be made easily by simple examination of psychologically important behavior.

Major genes and polygenes.   Current genetic theory distinguishes between *major genes* and *polygenes*. Major genes are regarded as mediating certain developmental processes more or less by their single influence, whereas polygenes are assumed to have cumulative effects upon a developmental process such that each has the same additive influence as any other does. Huntington's chorea provides us with an example of the influence of a major gene. The parent with a gene for Huntington's chorea will, on a probability basis, transmit the gene for the disease to one-half of his offspring. These children will receive a normal gene from the other parent but will develop the disease because the gene for it will dominate the normal gene with which it is paired. In a case such as this, the pathological gene is referred to as *dominant,* while the normal gene is termed *recessive.* Many pathological genes are presumed to be recessive and would not lead to appearance of the characteristic except in the case of the offspring of parents who both carry the gene. In this case, we would expect one-fourth of the offspring to exhibit the characteristic, this being the proportion in whom we could expect the pairing of both recessive genes to occur randomly.

However, much pathological behavior is not of the all-or-none variety, as can be seen in the case of Huntington's chorea, but may range with many gradations between nonexistence of such traits to presence to a very marked degree. The same is true for many human physical traits, such as height or hair color. To account for these characteristics, it appears plausible to assume the presence of polygenes which may combine cumulatively to determine the degree to which the characteristic appears in the offspring. The method of combination and addition is assumed to be the same as that for major genes, but the large number of genes of equivalent value for any given trait permits a larger number of gradations in the offspring.

As we have already seen, the most common assumption about gene action is that the effects are produced by means of aberrations in enzyme activity, which, in turn, are likely to give rise to pathologies of metabolism. Recent evidence suggests that there are at least 20 diseases of metabolism which are now known to have a hereditary origin and which have perceptible effects upon brain and behavior.

Porphyria, for example, is an inherited disorder of metabolism in which the clinical picture includes severe pain varying in location in any part of the nervous system, central, peripheral, or visceral, and frequently leading to an initial diagnosis of hysteria. During acute attacks, behavior may occur that is reminiscent of manic-depressive, hysterical, or Korsakoff's disorders. There is often evidence of lowered consciousness and schizophrenic-like hallucinations. *Porphyrins* are intermediate substances involved in the metabolism of certain essential bodily products, and deficiencies in porphyrin action will, in turn, lead to deficiencies in the metabolism of these products. Here, however, we see a disorder in which the underlying enzymatic pathology is fairly clearly identified. Many other kinds of behavior disorder may have genetic origins in which polygenic influences are important. When this is the case, the tracing down of specific enzyme deficiencies may be next to impossible.

Bearing these general comments in mind, we may now consider the research methods employed in the study of genetic factors in human psychopathology.

THE TWIN METHOD

The twin method is based upon the assumption (sufficiently validated to be treated as a fact) that there are two kinds of twins. One kind, known as *identical* or *monozygotic* (MZ), results from the splitting of a single fertilized ovum and hence, the two individuals have identical genetic endowments. A second kind of twin, *fraternal* or *dizygotic* (DZ), results from the simultaneous fertilization of two separate ova, and thus the resulting twins are only as alike genetically as any two siblings born of the same parents—the fact of their simultaneous conception does not increase their genetic identity beyond that level.

Since sex is genetically determined, MZ twins are always of the same sex, while DZ twins may be of the same sex or of different sexes. There is some possibility that there may be a rare occurrence of MZ twins who are not completely identical genetically. However, the incidence of this is so rare as to render it negligible as a factor influencing the assumptions of twin research.

Environment and genetics in twin behavior. The possible logical deductions to be drawn from the study of MZ- and DZ-twin comparisons are considerable. Some of the major deductions cited by Gottesman and Shields (1966) are among the following:

1.   Should there be no genetic factor of importance in producing a pattern of psychopathology, such as schizophrenia, and the major influence be from the environment, then there should be no significant difference in the rates of this disorder in the co-twins of affected MZ- and DZ-twin patients.

2.   If there are important genetic factors in schizophrenia (for example), then the incidence of it in the co-twins of affected patients should be higher than for the co-twins of DZ patients. This deduction is subject to the following limitations.

   a.   The deduction is limited if it can be shown that for some reason MZ twins are naturally more predisposed to the disorder than DZ twins.

   b.   The deduction is limited if it can be shown that the environments of MZ twins are more alike than those of DZ twins in the aspects that have been demonstrably proved to have etiological significance in the genesis of the disorder.

3.   Given that there is a higher incidence of an illness in MZ co-twins than in DZ twins, and the genetic factor is thus established, the cases among MZ twins where the co-twin did not contract the disorder can be studied for clues to those factors, perhaps environmental, that might operate prophylactically against the development of the disorder.

4.   By the same token, the symptom patterns that show the highest incidence of genetic influence might be examined with a view to identifying subtypes of the disorder that may have more genetic variance than other subtypes. In general, the possibility of developing new classification systems on a genetic basis can be envisaged.

In the absence of clear evidence that one or both of these limitations exist for the disorder in question, then the genetic hypothesis would be the most likely explanation of any higher rate in the MZ-twin pairs.

Concepts and terms in the twin method.   One of the major assumptions made in twin research is that when a disorder has a substantial genetic origin, this will show up in the higher likelihood that individuals with genetic similarity to a known patient will have the same disorder as the patient. Since MZ twins have 100 percent overlap in their genetic constitutions, when a given disorder has a purely genetic etiology we should expect complete agreement in their histories of this disorder; i.e., if one twin is free from the disorder, so should the other twin be, while if one twin has the disorder, so should the other. The percentage of agreement between the history of one twin and that of the other in a group of twins is known as the rate of *concordance*. Actually, the calculation of concordance rates is a complex matter, as we shall see shortly. For the moment, however, this description will serve for definition purposes.

In conducting twin research, it is usual to search some population of people who suffer from the disorder being investigated in order to find all patients who are twins. When such a patient is found, he is termed the *index case* or *proband*. His twin is then termed the *co-twin*. It is obvious that, when one twin has been hospitalized in a particular community, it is likely that his co-twin will be found in the same hospital if he is suffering from the same disorder. Thus, the co-twin of each member of the pair is also a proband in his own right. If we counted both twins as probands and then as co-twins, we would find a higher rate of concordance than we would by including any one of them only as a proband or a co-twin but not both. For example, if we found only three twins in a hospital, two of them being twins of each other, then we might find, by counting both that there were three probands, two of them with co-twins who had the same disorder. This would give a concordance rate of 66 percent. If we counted only one member of the hospitalized pair, then we would get a rate of only 50 percent. To surmount this difficulty, many investigators have preferred to use the pair as the base datum and hence refer to the *index pair* rather than the index case.

Returning to the term "concordance," we should note the variations in technique involved in its computation. The most limiting definition of concordance would be that the co-twin of a proband was (1) at the time of the investigation, (2) hospitalized with an identical diagnosis, characterized by (3) the same degree of severity of pathology. The least restrictive definition would be that the co-twin had (1) at some time in his life (2) been diagnosed as suffering from a disorder of the same general class as that of the proband. It will be clear that the less limiting the definition, the more likely it is that concordance rates will be high. The definition of concordance used will depend upon the kind of genetic hypothesis the investigator wishes to test and upon his conception of the disorder. Thus, if the researcher believes that schizophrenia is a disorder which may have long periods of arrest or remission, he will be willing to include any past history of a schizophrenic diagnosis in the co-twin as evidence of concordance. On the other hand, if he thinks that the disorder occurs only during a very limited part of the life-span, he may conclude his investigation with a much lower concordance rate.

By the same token, if he defines schizophrenia, for example, as including any of the four or five classical diagnostic categories plus diagnoses such as "schizoid personality" or "schizotype," he will probably find higher concordances than an investigator who is willing to count concordance only when both twins have an identical diagnosis in detail; e.g., both are diagnosed as "catatonic" or "paranoid" schizophrenic.

Methodological problems in twin research. Twin researchers face several important methodological difficulties in their work which are worthy of note at this point. Let us look at some of the major problems.

1. *Zygosity diagnosis.* Decisions that twins are MZ or DZ cannot be made reliably from judgments of their similarity of appearance. Recent work in biology has led to the discovery that many kinds of blood and serum groups are determined by genetic factors and that blood-typing thus provides one way to establish zygosity. With this as a comparison, judgments of similarity made from photographs produce only 78 percent correct conclusions (Gottesman, 1963). Other methods used include fingerprint ridge counts (Slater, 1963), eye-color similarity, and parental judgments. At present, blood-typing is regarded as the most fundamental method of establishing zygosity.

2. *Age corrections.* If an investigator draws a sample of twins, most of whom are in their early twenties, while studying a disease that continues to have high rates of onset until the late forties, he will be likely to estimate lower concordance rates than someone who works with a sample mostly in the fifty-year age range. Accordingly, it is necessary to make allowances (i.e., to "correct") for the empirical probability that an individual might exhibit the disorder at the age at which he is being studied. Several kinds of age correction may be applied (Strömgren, 1935; Weinberg, 1901), each with some limitations in specific kinds of sample. However, the main point to note here is that concordances may be compared only when the samples of MZ and DZ have the same age distributions and/or when the appropriate age corrections have been applied.

3. *Diagnosis of psychopathology.* We are already familiar with the serious problem of the reliability and validity of current diagnostic classifications. Since the same patient may be diagnosed as schizophrenic by one psychiatrist and as something else by another psychiatrist within a period of a few weeks (sometimes days), then we should find less than 100 percent concordance for the presence of a diagnosed disorder when the proband and the control are the same person! One partial solution to this problem is for the investigator to arrange to have the diagnoses repeated on both probands and co-twins by a single diagnostic procedure with some standard criteria. This may reduce the interrater unreliability but will not eliminate the subtle variance that may creep in when the investigator himself is deciding upon the diagnosis and already has a hypothesis (genetic or environmental) at stake. An alternative solution is to use some more objective diagnostic device (such as the MMPI, a standardized form of case history or behavior checklist, a specific set of measurable deficiencies that may be quantified) and have it applied blindly by a technician unaware of the diagnosis of the proband.

4. *The social environment of twins.* There is some possibility that the social environments of identical twins are more nearly alike than those of DZ twins and especially than those of opposite-sexed DZ twins. Thus, there is always a risk that the higher concordance rate that may be found in the MZ twins is at least in part a reflection of more concordant environments. Methodologically speaking, the best solution to this problem is to be found in the analysis of concordance rates for twins separated and reared apart from an early age. Such controls are not readily to be had for the asking, however, and this is clearly evident in the research literature, which contains relatively few such twin sets. In the meantime, we should note that there seems to be low plausibility to the suggestion that the environments of DZ twins of the same sex are as discordant as their genetic endowments are, and thus the investigator is placed in the position of weighing plausibility rather than of hoping for precise measurements of environmental similarity.

FAMILY STUDIES

Genetic investigators have also turned their attention to the concordance rates for psychopathology to be found in members of the same family with varying degrees of kinship to the proband patient. These empirical concordance rates may be evaluated against various theoretical assumptions. If we assume complete genetic determination of a disorder, then we should expect the relatives of patients to exhibit the disorder in proportion to the similarity of their genetic endowments to that of the patient proband. Thus, monozygotic twins would have 100 percent concordance, full siblings would have 50 percent overlap of genetic constitution and, hence, 50 percent concordance, etc. However, this would be the case only when the disorder is presumed to follow a simple Mendelian model whereby the gene for the disorder is dominant. When the gene is recessive, the expectation that schizophrenic behavior would occur would be reduced. Theoretical expectancies for various degrees of kinship are shown in Table 6-1, both dominant and recessive models being assumed; the empirical findings are also shown for comparison purposes.

However, the probability that schizophrenia is to be explained in terms of simple genetic models such as dominant- or recessive-gene loadings is slight, and polygenic models are more favored by behavior geneticists. The figure should be regarded as illustrative of a principle rather than as demonstrative of the validity of any Mendelian model.

LONGITUDINAL HIGH-RISK STUDIES

Establishing concordance rates for existing probands with a diagnosis of psychopathology tests the validity of the hypothesis of genetic etiology. It does not, however, provide us with any ready clues about the psychological or biological processes that are being determined genetically and that will finally develop into the psychopathological pattern. In order to study the preclinical manifestations of a disorder, it is necessary to have some way of identifying a high-risk population whose members are as yet too young to present the overt symptomatology of the disorder. This technique is of fairly recent development in psychopathological research. A good example is provided by the work of Mednick and Schulsinger (1965). They selected a sample of children between the ages of ten and eighteen whose mothers had a history of hospitalization for schizophrenia. Examination of Table 6-1 above would indicate an empirical probability that 16.4 percent of those children would receive a diagnosis of schizophrenia in adult life. The sample was collected in Copenhagen, and a preliminary check of empirical probabilities found in earlier Danish work showed a risk of 12.7 percent, fairly close to the 16.4 percent predicted from accumulated studies elsewhere. A group of

Table 6.1   Risk of Schizophrenia for Relatives of Schizophrenics: Empirical and Mendelian Theoretical Expectancy

		Theoretical expectancy	
Class	Percentage risk of schizophrenia	Completely dominant gene	Completely recessive gene
Children of two nonschizophrenic parents (general population)	0.9		
Relatives of adult schizophrenic index cases—			
Not consanguineous			
Step-sibs	1.8		
Spouse	2.1		
First cousins	2.6	.13	.03
Nephews and nieces	3.9	.25	.05
Grandchildren	4.3		
Half-sibs	7.1	.25	.15
Parents	9.2	.50	.09
Full-sibs	14.2	.50	.30
Dizygotic co-twins	14.5	.50	.30
Dizygotic co-twins of same sex	17.6	.50	.30
Children with one schizophrenic parent	16.4	.50	
Children with two schizophrenic parents	68.1	.75	1.00
Monozygotic co-twins	86.2	1.00	1.00
Monozygotic co-twins living apart for at least five years	77.6	1.00	1.00
Monozygotic co-twins not so separated	91.5	1.00	1.00

Source: After Gregory (1960); Kallmann (1946, 1950); Shields & Slater (1960).

high-risk children was obtained in this way and matched with a group of control children. Matching was achieved on the basis of sex, age, father's occupation, rural or urban residence, years of education, and upbringing in own home or in an institution. All subjects were then studied by a variety of techniques. Autonomic responsiveness (which we have already seen in Chapter 5 to be an important concern in investigations of schizophrenia) was recorded. Conditioning and stimulus generalization were investigated—as our earlier discussion in Chapter 4 would lead us to expect. A variety of other measures included personality tests such as the MMPI, adjective checklists, and word association procedures.

At the time these measurements were made, all children in both groups were behaviorally normal. Arrangements were then made throughout Denmark for the investigators to be informed whenever any child in the study came into the hands of a hospital, physician, public agency, police, etc., for deviant behavior. At the time of writing, several of the high-risk children have already been located in this way. When the number who develop disorders is sufficiently large to permit statistical comparisons to be made, it will then be possible to examine the early data to see if differences existed at that point in time. These differences should then provide clues to the psychological processes being affected genetically in the transmission of schizophrenia.

POPULATION STUDIES

Another set of methods depends upon the study of the presence of a disorder in an entire population. For obvious reasons, such populations must be small enough to be enumerated, isolated enough to reduce the probability that immigration and emigration will seriously alter the population composition in a short time, and well enough served that any case of the disorder is likely to be diagnosed as such and recorded somewhere.

Geneticists make use of certain concepts in approaching this kind of study. The first is the notion of *incidence*. Incidence may be defined as the number of *new cases* of a disorder that develop in a given period of time per unit of the population. It is customary to use one year as the period of time, and 100,000 as the population base. Thus, we may compute incidence with the aid of the following equation:

$$\text{Incidence} = \frac{\text{number of new cases developed in one year}}{\text{number of base population}} \times 100,000$$

The base population may be any sample of interest such as all the members of a given village, an age group, or an income group.

Prevalence of a disorder refers not to a rate but to a ratio. It is defined as the proportion of a base population who had the disorder on a selected date (hypothetically on a selected moment in time). Here again, it is customary to report the ratio on the basis of 100,000 population units.

$$\text{Prevalence} = \frac{\text{number of cases existing on a given date}}{\text{number of base population}} \times 100,000$$

Since different investigators tend to prefer one method of computation over the other, it is necessary to know which is being used when one result is compared with another. Incidences and prevalences may be calculated for any kind of population or time unit pertinent to the problem at hand.

With these terms in hand, we may now look at some of the major methodological problems involved in population studies.

Population drift. An ideal population for study would be one in which the pedigree of each member is known, there is no inward or outward migration, and the environment does not change significantly from one generation to the next. Under these circumstances we should then need some comprehensive record of the prevalence of the disorder in question at some earlier generation and the records of its occurrence in each case since then. In practice, it is difficult, perhaps impossible, to meet any of these requirements completely. Isolated communities are likely to be rural; the population is likely to drift out of the community towards the urban areas; those who successfully emigrate are not likely to have many cases of handicapping psychopathology and thus the direction of drift is not random as to probable genetic composition. In urban areas, it is possible that the psychopathologically handicapped will sink in the social scale owing to occupational incompetence, and thus over several generations a class difference will be apparent in the prevalence of the disorder. What is then unresolved is whether the conditions of life in the lower social class produce the disorder (a predominantly environmental explanation) or whether genetic inferiority tends to push people into the class (a mainly genetic explanation).

The first of these explanations hinges upon the demonstration that there are sets of psychologically stressful events occurring in lower-class life that are quite independent of the behaviors of the members of the class. Although, generally speaking, no investigator has yet been able to separate clearly the effects of personal inadequacy from the effects of the environmental quality of lower socioeconomic circumstances, some aspects of the latter seem fairly evident. Early deaths of infants and young adults are more frequent in lower-income groups and bring attendant psychological stress to the surviving family. Stability of employment is often less dependent upon individual ability than upon seasonal and accidental fluctuations in the economy of the society at large—hence the stresses of unemployment are likely to impinge on members of this class regardless of personal resourcefulness. Since immigrants are more likely to enter the country as members of low-income groups and to become residents of low-income areas, the problems of ethnic conflict are most likely to be found in these areas. In recent years, the disturbing influence of relocation programs as part of urban renewal has been directed more or less exclusively at low-income areas. To put the matter tersely, poverty brings stresses to anyone, regardless of his personal psychological resources. Riches, as the witticism goes, may not bring happiness, but they enable the wealthy to be miserable in comfort!

Although all of the foregoing is true—and to a large extent, simply a statement of the obvious—it is equally true that psychological inadequacy is likely to lead to a drift downward in socioeconomic status. It is very difficult for an ambulatory schizophrenic to become or remain an executive in a corporation or, indeed, to hold any kind of well-paying employment. All in all, it is difficult to doubt that some percentage of the difficulties found disproportionately in lower-income groups represents the effects of *social drift* downward. The question of interest is, how big this percentage is. We have few data on social drift. We are unsure, for example, how many schizophrenic patients currently in a lower-income group were once of higher socioeconomic status or had parents of higher socioeconomic status. Without data of this kind it is impossible to come to any reasonable assessment of the relative effects of social drift versus environmental stress in lower-income-disorder frequencies.

Diagnostic criteria. In a population with heterogeneous subpopulations, it is more than probable that the criteria for diagnosing a disorder will differ from one group to the next. What may appear to be psychotic in a lower-middle-class subject may appear to be a harmless eccentricity in the wealthy. Even apart from gross discrepancies of this kind, we have already seen earlier in this book that professional clinicians diagnosing the same patient may have serious disagreements. An example of the problem of definition is to be found in the classic work of Hollingshead and Redlich (1958) on the frequency of mental illness in various social classes in New Haven, Connecticut. Their definition of mental illness is given as follows:

> Any person in treatment with a psychiatrist or under the care of a psychiatric clinic or mental hospital between May 31 and December 1, 1950 who was a resident of New Haven . . . . A "psychiatrist" is a person who holds a Doctor of Medicine degree and has completed or is undergoing training in a psychiatric hospital or clinic in accordance with the criteria of the medical profession . . . . In so rigidly defining a case, we have not counted a significant percentage of mentally ill persons who are in a therapeutic relationship with physicians other than psychiatrists, psychologists, psychiatric social workers and other accredited persons or agencies . . . . Although such "patients" pose an important question for investigation, we do not consider it desirable or feasible to include them in this study [p. 19].

Dohrenwend and Dohrenwend (1967) have pointed out that this problem is most likely to be exacerbated when the diagnosis is of a general personality disorder rather than when it is a question of diagnosing psychosis. Personality disorders, they point out, are most likely to be defined in terms of socially unacceptable behavior rather than of more conventional psychopathological criteria. For example, in one study (Roth & Luton, 1943) cases were included on the basis of "symptoms" such as unacceptable use of tobacco and of miscegenation! Another example is provided by the fact that in one part of the United States there was a reported drop in the rate of psychopathic personality from 13 per 10,000 to 5.2 per 10,000 in the period 1933–1936. This remarkable reduction in psychopathology was explained by Lemkau (1949) as due to the tendency of the people conducting the survey early in the depression years to regard unemployment as evidence of psychopathic personality. Three years later, they revised their opinion on this matter when they had recognized the extent to which lack of employment was a worldwide problem not properly attributable to the psyches of the unemployed.

Quite apart from the fact that standards for diagnosis may vary from one class to another and that the definition of a "patient" may be made arbitrarily as in the case above, there is yet a third problem. This is the fact that many potential patients may never be available for diagnosis, because of different class habits regarding self-referral for psychological difficulties. Poorer people may hesitate to go to a physician at all, and especially to a psychiatrist, preferring to cope with their difficulties as best they can. In principle, the only method of dealing with this source of bias is to make an assessment of the whole sample under investigation. Such a procedure was used, for example, by Essen-Möller (1956) in his investigation of the prevalence of personality problems in the population of a Swedish village. Here the research team conducted a diagnostic interview with every member of the population—although the conditions under which some of these were done (on the doorstep, in fields) raise questions about their validity and reliability.

Accuracy of records. It is almost axiomatic that general hospital records are rarely designed for use for research purposes. Many kinds of information that may be of use in later research are either not recorded at all or are recorded casually and unreliably. Important demographic data such as date of birth, premorbid occupation, and level of education are recorded as told by family informants and rarely checked directly from the archives of employers, schools, and so on. Compulsory recording of the date of birth is a relatively recent development in many countries, and records of births before the twentieth century are often in error or lacking entirely. Records of the date and cause of death are also open to question in many cases. When the cause of death, such as death by suicide, is likely to be an embarrassment to the surviving family, there are probabilities that a sympathetic family physician will record the death as an accident or as due to some other more acceptable cause. Countries vary in the care and accuracy with which records are kept. Scandinavian countries are generally more efficient in this respect than

American or other European nations—which is one of the reasons why genetic and demographic methods have been more widely and successfully applied there.

Cross-cultural generalizations. When a population is found that approximates the requirements for a suitable sample to study, the next problem arises when we attempt to apply the findings to another culture. Environmental stress in a society that is isolated and simple will differ from that found in a modern, open, and complex culture. When the genetic hypothesis at issue is one that includes reference to the interaction of hereditary factors with environmental stress, it becomes difficult to apply the findings in one kind of environment to the problem of prediction of the incidence of the disorder in a different environment. Under these circumstances, the findings in the simple culture may be used to help establish the validity of the basic genetic hypothesis; they are less amenable to an understanding of the distribution and incidence of the overt disorder in a group of more complex societies.

Good illustrations of these difficulties have been reported by Dohrenwend and Dohrenwend (1965). Reviewing many studies of social class and behavioral disorder, they find that in the investigations in which untreated as well as treated cases are included, the percentages of disorder found in total communities have ranged from as low as 1 percent to as high as 60 percent. Although the rates reported from Asia are invariably lower than those reported from Western regions (3.0 percent reported from Tokyo is the highest Asian figure while 64 percent from a Canadian fishing village is the highest Western figure in their survey), the rates reported from Africa are also very high (40–45 percent). Hence, it is not possible to conclude, by comparing their rates of disorder with those for primitive societies, that the residents of complex Western societies have been demonstrated to be more susceptible.

Their survey further shows that the percentages of psychological disorder found tend to increase when the investigator uses techniques involving more contact with the subject population. Thus, rates computed by reference to records and from informants yield lower values than those obtained by direct interview and examination of every member of the population.

Clearly, the incidence of disorder cannot be regarded as a naturally increasing function of the "westernization" of a culture. The kind of judgment involved in calling one culture "simple" and another "complex" is itself a rather dubious estimate of the probable intensity of psychological stresses in the cultures so described.

Genetics, diagnosis, and behavioral units. Earlier in this chapter, we saw that the most probable mode of influence of genetic factors is through the mediation of enzyme-metabolism relationships. The manner in which a deficiency of metabolism produces a particular pattern of disordered behavior is far from clear. Nor is it clear that disorders of metabolism will produce patterns of disorder corresponding to those defined in current systems of psychiatric taxonomy. It is more likely that hereditary mechanisms will produce, for example, differences in the lability of response in the autonomic nervous system. These, in turn, may tend to produce any one of several kinds of overt patterns of disordered behavior, depending mainly upon the kind of environmental experience that has occurred to the individual. By the same token, a given pattern of disorder may be generated by other combinations of genetic-experiential events. When this happens, the discovery of a "pure" genetic influence may be difficult. On the other hand, if the investigation had been directed to measures of autonomic functioning directly, rather than to its second-order effects in complex behavior, the nature of the underlying genetic patterns might be much more obvious. The approach of Mednick and Schulsinger (1965), already mentioned in this chapter, is an example of the recognition of this problem.

Comparative Epidemiology

So far we have been concerned more or less exclusively with methods of investigating genetic hypotheses. However, many problems related to cultural differences in the incidence and prevalence of psychopathology have no direct genetic implications. Rather they are concerned with the effect of different environments upon the occurrence of psychopathology. These studies of comparative epidemiology face methodological problems also, of which the following are among the most important.

1. *Differential reporting.* From one country to another, and often within the same country, the method of reporting an "admission" varies considerably. Thus, in some cases, admission as a bed-occupying

inpatient is necessary for an admission to be recorded while in others the diagnosis of psychopathology is regarded as an "admission," even if treatment is never undertaken or is provided on an outpatient basis.

2. *Diagnostic classification system.* In 1948, the World Health Organization introduced an international scheme for classifying psychopathology in the expectation that its use in all countries would lead to greater comparability in epidemiologic studies, in communication about research or clinical cases, etc. Twelve years later, Meyer (1960) reported that it was then in use only in Finland, Greece, Great Britain, Ireland, Yugoslavia, Portugal, Hungary, and in some hospitals in Holland and Peru. It had not been adopted in the United States, Scandinavia, the Soviet Union, and many other large countries. Comparative statements about the incidence of particular kinds of psychopathology from one culture to another are, therefore, difficult to make with any assurance of validity.

3. *Differential detection and hospitalization techniques.* Countries and states differ widely in the availability of mental health personnel—there being generally more of these people as a percentage of the population in urban and highly developed areas than in rural or primitive areas. Since the detection of psychopathology depends at some point on the presence of a qualified individual to make the diagnosis and initiate treatment, the incidence of psychopathology will often seem to be low in areas where the problem is the lack of facilities to detect and treat it.

In computing rates of hospitalization—and particularly prevalence figures—an additional problem is posed by the differences in release practices from one place to another. Kramer, Pollack, and Rednick (1961), for example, studied the probability of release from the hospital after a first admission as a function of the number of months since the admission and of the state in which the hospital was located. Using a group of states that employed the same standard reporting procedure, they found that, during the year 1954, nearly 50 percent of first admissions to Arkansas hospitals had been released 12 months later, while the comparable figures from other states such as Illinois (20 percent), New York (14 percent), and Indiana (11 percent) were markedly lower. It is clear that low rates of release, unless accompanied by relatively high rates of admission, mean that the chronicity of hospital populations will vary significantly from state to state. By the same token, if prevalence figures are based upon resident hospital populations, then the prevalence rates in states with early-release policies will appear much lower than the rates in states with slow-release policies. Unless it is assumed that early release is mainly a consequence of successful therapy, it is not possible to make valid comparisons of prevalence without knowledge of the release rates.

Of necessity, the kind of data obtainable from population studies is broad-gauge. The environmental stresses and the genetic composition of whole populations are difficult to estimate in other than the crudest terms. In our discussion of the ulcer study in Chapter 1, we saw that, for example, the stress of life for a military recruit is not the same for all individuals. Although it produced the expected stress response from a sufficient number of subjects to permit the hypothesis to be supported, there were many subjects for whom the predicted consequences did not materialize. Consequently, investigators have also turned to more detailed examination of the psychological environments of patients. Chief among the foci of interest of these investigations is the matter of family interaction and parent-patient relationships. We shall now look at these rather briefly.

FAMILY STUDIES

Studies of family interaction have generally been initiated with a specific hypothesis in mind. The hypotheses have usually been that there is maternal overprotection, parental friction, incongruity of parent-child communication, etc. Hypotheses of this kind require the use of some measuring procedure with which to quantify "overprotection," "friction," or whatever the interaction variable is believed to be. Since the investigator cannot produce the variable experimentally, his techniques of control are limited. He may simply take samples from the appropriate situation (e.g., parents talking to each other as an opportunity to observe the spontaneous occurrence of "friction") or he may create situations in which the crucial behavior should emerge (e.g., provoking discussion of controversial topics between parents to see if "friction" will ensue).

Not surprisingly, the major problems of methodology are to be found in the techniques of observation employed. Let us look at some of them here.

Retrospective accounts. Sometimes an investigator uses parental recollections as the basis for his assessment of parent-child relationships in the early life of the patient. Unfortunately, it is more than possible that recollection of early childhood events by a parent is related to overprotectiveness. The mother who is unusually involved with her child's development, health, activities, etc., is likely to keep souvenirs, records, school reports, medical data, and so on. Thus, fullness and accuracy of recall are likely to be confounded with overprotection. Should the investigator decide to confine his study to the parents who can give him enough data to make a judgment about their overprotectiveness, he is likely to emerge with an unusually high proportion of overprotective parents in his sample. An example of this is to be found in an early study by Kasanin, Knight, and Sage (1934), who examined the hospital records of schizophrenics. Confining themselves to those cases wherein the parental behavior was well-documented (based on parental reports to the hospital authority), they discovered that 60 percent of the patients exhibited parental overprotection. Since they did not have a control group of nonpatients or of poorly documented patients, it is difficult to know what these results might mean. Nevertheless, it led them to hypothesize that overprotection was important in the development of schizophrenia.

Some improvement may be made by the use of objective measures of early home environment—such as unemployment frequency, deaths in the family, and parental separations. Here again, however, if the data are inferred from records, the problem of selectivity in record keeping may still exist.

Current behavior. When the investigator observes current behavior, the major problem is access to a suitable sample. Parents are often unwilling to cooperate in research that focuses attention on their own possible contribution to the psychopathology of their child. Hence, parents who do cooperate may not provide a representative sample. Even when parents and patients do agree to assist in research, they do so with an awareness that their behavior is under scrutiny, an awareness that may lead them to be on their "best" behavior during the study. This, of course, may bias results seriously.

Sometimes bias may be used to advantage by an ingenious investigator. Hotchkiss, Carman, Ogilby, and Wiesenfeld (1955) studied the "overprotection" hypothesis in the mothers of schizophrenic patients. They observed the behavior of 22 mothers of schizophrenic sons who regularly visited their sons on the hospital wards. It seems reasonable to assume that mothers who visit their schizophrenic sons are more over-protective than those who do not. In spite of this obvious bias in favor of the hypothesis, the investigators found that only three of the mothers exhibited the expected characteristics. Under the circumstances, the lack of a standard control group would have weakened findings in favor of the hypothesis, but it does not weaken their actual conclusion that the overprotection hypothesis is unsupported.

Given that an appropriate sample may be found, the next problem for the investigator is the rather typical one of the reliability and validity of his measures of interaction. In principle, these problems are no different from those discussed already in Chapter 1. However, in practice it appears that dependence upon pure clinical impression has persisted longer in the study of family interaction than in the direct study of individual patients. We shall not repeat them again here but may make the point by illustrations from the literature of the study of the families of schizophrenics. Sanua (1967) quotes an Argentinian psychiatrist, trained in the United States, reporting on the occurrence of autistic children in the Argentine.

> I was able to see here and in Kansas City the schizophrenic mother-child dyad, the symbiotic type of problem, and the three types described by L. Bender, plus the autistic child. However, this last entity is not frequent in this country. I have no statistics to prove what I am saying, and I am only giving you an impression of my clinical experience . . . [p. 173].

The literature is replete with studies in which the investigator was "able to see" the kind of family interaction that his theoretical predilections led him to expect. Tietze (1949) interviewed the mothers of 25 schizophrenics. Of these, she found 10 mothers overtly rejecting their children, and the remaining 15 were more "subtle" in their rejection. She also found them overanxious, domineering, restrictive, and sexually frigid. Since Tietze herself did the interviewing, did not interview any control parents, and was in favor of the hypothesis from the outset, it is difficult to interpret her data.

Parent availability.   For obvious reasons, it is easier to enlist the co-operation of mothers than of fathers in this kind of research. Unless the investigator is willing and able to conduct his research outside normal working hours, many fathers simply cannot attend the hospital to participate. Consequently, the data available are heavily skewed toward a focus on the role of the mother in the genesis of schizophrenia. A proper evaluation of the role of a particular parent clearly requires the presence of both parents in the samples and their observation by equally comprehensive means. Failing this kind of control, it is not surprising if the role of the father in the family appears "passive" to the investigator: the very fact of the father's unavailability for research may easily be interpreted to mean that he is relatively uninvolved in the affairs of the family and presumably a passive participant in their development.

Child-rearing practices. Investigation of child-rearing practices as antecedents to psychopathology is, perhaps, one of the thorniest areas of behavioral research. Strictly speaking, the ideal research procedure would be one in which the manner of raising the child is observed and quantified directly by the investigator. Data based upon patient's report, parents' reports, or recall by either of these sources, are notoriously liable to error. On the other hand, for obvious reasons, adequate observation of child-rearing practices as they are being applied is very hard to achieve. Even when access to the home is permitted, there is the strong possibility that the behavior of the parents is modified by their knowledge that they are being observed.

If, somehow, these difficulties can be overcome, the second requirement is that the child-rearing practices should be shown to *antedate* the development of the psychopathology. This means that it is necessary to investigate very large samples of families and wait for some of the children in them to develop psychopathology. This kind of study has not yet been conducted, and in the overwhelming majority of investigations the families chosen for observation have been selected because one or more children have already developed psychopathology.

When this is the case, the basic problem is whether the behavior of the parents is largely a consequence of the difficult behavior of their child, or vice versa. For instance, let us turn to a study by Behrens and Goldfarb (1958) of the family environment of schizophrenic children:

The child was handled with an exaggerated degree of tentativeness, often accompanied by overinvolvement in the child's activities. The mother, in particular, gave the impression that she felt any misstep would result in an uncontrollable situation, and seemed harassed in her effort to comply with the demands of the child and to keep things on an even keel [p. 310].

The important thing to keep in mind here is that these are children who have been found so difficult to control that the parents have been driven to the drastic step of seeking aid from psychiatrists. It seems difficult to imagine that the investigators could really have expected to find parental behavior other than that described!

Some investigators who feel that early psychotic disturbances in children have a predominantly biological origin point to the similarity in the reactions of parents of children with established physical illness. Such a study was reported by Fitzelle (1959) testing the hypothesis that childhood asthma is a consequence of specific parental attitudes. By comparing the parents of asthmatic children with those of children with a history of physical illness, he was able to demonstrate that the attitudes of both are the same but that their attitudes differ from those of parents of well children. Anxiety, overprotection, and the like, are very reasonable responses on the part of a parent to the presence of a sick child.

In spite of this, Boatman and Szurek (1960), for example, claim that "the etiology of psychotic disorders of childhood is entirely psychogenic." They believe that the child's reaction is a psychotic exaggeration of the mother's basic traits—the extreme tension of the psychotic child is an exaggeration of the anxiety of the mother, etc. They point out that it was most difficult to conduct psychotherapy with these mothers in view of the mothers' conviction that their children had an organic illness! Since the writers had not systematically compared the behavior of these mothers with that of mothers of children with organic illnesses, it is difficult to see how they could dismiss the organic hypothesis so cavalierly.

Escalona (1948), for example, commenting on the probability of a biological origin for childhood psychosis, stated:

> Whenever the life histories of severely disorganized children were given adequate scrutiny, it was noted that disturbances in the earliest and most basic interpersonal relationships were present . . . . Furthermore, most of the mothers, and other persons in close contact with these children, spontaneously commented that there was something puzzling and "different" about these children from a very early age on [p. 127].

Although it is quite possible that careful scrutiny of cases will produce whatever evidence the scrutinizer is seeking, Escalona's observations provide an excellent illustration of the dangers that arise when the researcher assumes in advance that parents' behavior causes children's psychopathology.

Class differences.   Once again, the factor of class differences may operate to produce spurious correlations between child-rearing practices and psychopathology. To put the matter simply, membership in the lower socioeconomic class may be accompanied by exposure to many stresses—as we have seen already. Membership in this class may also be accompanied by certain practices in child rearing. Although the stresses may be responsible for the subsequent appearance of psychopathology, the investigator may be looking only at correlations with child-rearing practices. He will find significant correlations and run the risk of interpreting them as evidence in favor of his hypothesis that the stresses produce the psychopathology.

The appropriate controls for this kind of confounding are relatively easy to apply but are often omitted. Class and ethnic origins should be matched in both pathological and control samples, with enough heterogeneity of both class and ethnic representation to permit generalization of the results beyond the limits of any single group. Failure to do this can produce the kind of results found by Despert (1938), who collected data on 29 children, mainly boys, admitted to the New York State Psychiatric Institute with a diagnosis of childhood schizophrenia. She found in 19 of the mothers signs of aggressiveness, overanxiety, and oversolicitousness, a more subdued role being played by the father. However, the majority of her group of parents were Jewish, and it is difficult to be sure that she was not describing a kind of mother-child relationship fairly normal in that ethnic group. No control subjects were observed and hence the results of the investigation are essentially meaningless.

Post hoc analysis.   Sometimes the investigator enters into the study of the family interaction of patients with the general hypothesis that it will be found to be unusual but without specifying how this will be exhibited. After the investigation is completed, the conclusion may be offered that some particular kind of deviant family interaction was present. The investigator did not commit himself beforehand to what

this would be and did not report the large number of potential devian-
cies looked for but not found. Consequently it is impossible to decide
whether his observations are significant or not. This is so, even when a
control group is used, as was discussed at length in our account of cross-
validity in Chapter 1 (see p. 21).

A clear example of this is to be seen in the well-known study of family
interaction in schizophrenia by Lidz and his associates at Yale (Lidz,
Cornelison, Fleck, and Terry, 1957; Lidz, Parker, & Cornelison, 1956).
They studied 14 families drawn predominantly from upper-middle or
upper-class families. This was a group mainly able to support a family
member in a private hospital for long periods of time. No control group
was used. From the 14 fathers observed, they emerged with a group of
no fewer than five possible pathogenic kinds of role that a father might
play. These included (1) fathers who are in severe conflict with their
wives and who try to win the daughter to their side; (2) fathers whose
hostility turns toward the children rather than toward the wives; (3)
fathers who have an exalted, grandiose concept of themselves; (4) fathers who scarcely participate in the rearing of their children; and (5)
fathers who act as siblings to their children and accept the domination
of the wife.

From such a diverse group of patterns found in so small a group, it
would seem most parsimonious to conclude that the notion of paternal
pathogenesis of schizophrenia is unsupported, or, better still, that the
study had provided a basis for making hypotheses but no evidence on
which to base a conclusion. This, however, turns out not to be the case,
and the study is widely cited in support of the belief that particular
kinds of paternal role are related to the genesis of schizophrenia.

We should note, in conclusion, that the methodological problems of
research into family interaction are basically the same as those that arise
in all kinds of behavioral research. They are the fundamental problems
of control, reliability, and objectivity of measurement, and of cautious
inference of causative relations when the investigator has not manipulated the supposed etiological variable. Sensitivity to these problems
has long been present in the work of experimental psychopathologists
working on questions of the behavior of individual patients but has been
somewhat slowly acquired by workers in the field of family interaction.
As is always the case, the presence of this kind of methodological weakness should not lead us to assume that the conclusions offered are neces-

sarily false. It should lead us to the more conservative view that they are, as yet, unproved.

Summary

Investigative techniques in psychopathology have spread beyond the clinic and the laboratory to include research in social and genetic influences in the behavior disorders. Consideration has been given in this chapter to genetic methods, including *twin* and *family-kinship* studies; epidemiologic approaches with their concomitant problems of *sampling* and *diagnostic reliability, cultural differences* in diagnostic practices, differential *detection, treatment, record-keeping* and *reporting* practices; etc. We have also looked at the developing work in family interaction and noted the problems of *behavioral measurement, sample bias, confoundings* between *class* and *child-rearing* practices, the prevailing *lack of control groups* and *cross-validation* procedures, etc.

Awareness of difficulties such as these, present in all areas of research into human behavior, should not discourage us from investigation. Rather, it should challenge us to resolve the difficulties with the consciousness that a single well-controlled study advancing our knowledge of psychopathology contributes more to the ultimate welfare of patients than all the published speculations do, however compassionate their purpose and however authoritative their tone.

SUGGESTED READINGS

General

1. Eysenck, H. J. (Ed.) *Handbook of abnormal psychology*. London: Sir Isaac Pitman, 1960. An advanced resource book covering major topics in abnormal psychology with an emphasis upon research data. Although it is somewhat advanced for the general undergraduate reader, it contains excellent illustrations of the overall research strategies with which important problems have been investigated.
2. Maher, B. A. *Principles of psychopathology*. New York: McGraw-Hill, 1966. A basic text, suitable for the undergraduate, presenting the subject matter of abnormal psychology from the point of view of experimental psychology and psychobiology.

Research and Scientific Method

3. Braithwaite, R. B. *Scientific explanation*. Cambridge: Cambridge University Press, 1953. An elementary but useful discussion of some of the functions of hypotheses, models, laws, and theories in scientific explanation.
4. Gottschalk, L. A., & Auerbach, A. H. *Methods of research in psychotherapy*. New York: Appleton-Century-Crofts, 1966. A collection of papers dealing with a variety of methodological and technical questions relevant to the investigation of psychotherapy.
5. Sidman, M. *Tactics of scientific research*. New York: Basic Books, 1960. A detailed account of the assumptions and method employed in research conducted in the operant-conditioning paradigm.
6. Wolman, B. B. (Ed.) *Handbook of clinical psychology*. New York: McGraw-Hill, 1965. Part I of this book is a collection of five

chapters dealing with research methods in clinical psychology. Included are discussions of the case method, experimental techniques, problems of measurement, and statistical techniques.

Resources for Subject Matter

7. DEESE, J., & HULSE, S. *The psychology of learning.* (3rd ed.). New York: McGraw-Hill, 1958. A basic coverage of the principles of learning. This is written very clearly and is suitable for the general reader.

8. DEUTSCH, J. A., & DEUTSCH, D. *Physiological psychology.* Homewood, Ill.: Dorsey Press, 1966. A comprehensive account of the principles and findings in the relationship between biology and behavior. Although presented from a particular viewpoint, this book is suitable as a general text.

9. GELLHORN, E., & LOOFBOURROW, G. N. *Emotions and emotional disorders.* New York: Harper & Row, 1963. Thorough discussion of biological systems in the human is provided along with data relating these systems to abnormal behavior.

REFERENCES

ACHINSTEIN, P.   Theoretical models. *British Journal of the Philosophy of Science,* 1965, **16,** 102–120.

AGNEW, N., & AGNEW, M.   Drive level effects on tasks of narrow and broad attention. *Quarterly Journal of Experimental Psychology,* 1963, **15,** 58–62.

ALLYON, T.   Intensive treatment of psychotic behavior by stimulus satiation. *Behavior Research and Therapy,* 1963, **1,** 53–61.

ASH, P.   The reliability of psychiatric diagnosis. *Journal of Abnormal and Social Psychology,* 1949, **44,** 272–277.

ATKINSON, J. W., & MCCLELLAND, D. C.   The projective expression of needs. II: The effect of different intensities of the hunger drive on thematic apperception. *Journal of Experimental Psychology,* 1948, **38,** 643–658.

AX, A. F.   The physiological differentiation between fear and anger in humans. *Psychosomatic Medicine,* 1953, **15,** 433–442.

BECK A. T.   Reliability of psychiatric diagnosis: A critique of systematic studies. *American Journal of Psychiatry,* 1962, **119,** 210–216.

BEHRENS, M. L., & GOLDFARB, W.   A study of patterns of interaction of families of schizophrenic children in residential treatment. *American Journal of Orthopsychiatry,* 1958, **28,** 300–312.

BLEULER, E.   *Dementia praecox, or the group of schizophrenias.* New York: International Universities Press, 1950.

BOATMAN, M. J., & SZUREK, S. A.   A clinical study of childhood schizophrenia. In D. D. Jackson (Ed.), *The etiology of schizophrenia.* New York: Basic Books, 1960.

BRAITHWAITE, R. B.   *Scientific explanation: A study of the function theory, probability and law in science.* Cambridge: Cambridge University Press, 1953.

BUSS, A. H.   *Psychopathology.* New York: Wiley, 1966.

BYRNE, D. Repression-sensitization as a dimension of personality. In B. A. Maher (Ed.), *Progress in experimental personality research. Vol. I.* New York: Academic Press, 1964. Pp. 169–220.

CAMERON, N. The functional psychoses. In J. McV. Hunt (Ed.), *Personality and the behavior disorders.* New York: Ronald Press, 1944.

CAMPBELL, D. T., & FISKE, D. F. Convergent and discriminant validation by the multi-trait, multi-method matrix. *Psychological Bulletin,* 1959, **56**, 81–105.

CLARK, W. C., BROWN, J. C., & RUTSCHMANN, J. Flicker sensitivity and response bias in psychiatric patients and normal subjects. *Journal of Abnormal Psychology,* 1967, **72**, 35–42.

CONGER, J. J. The effects of alcohol on conflict behavior in the albino rat. *Quarterly Journal of Studies in Alcohol,* 1951, **12**, 1–29.

CRIDER, A. B., GRINSPOON, L., & MAHER, B. A. Autonomic and psychomotor correlates of premorbid adjustment in schizophrenia. *Psychosomatic Medicine,* 1965, **27**, 201–206.

CRONBACH, L. J., & MEEHL, P. E. Construct validity in psychological tests. *Psychological Bulletin,* 1955, **52**, 281–302.

CRONHOLM, B., & BLOMQUIST, C. Memory disturbances after electroconvulsive therapy. 2. Conditions one week after a series of treatments. *Acta Psychiatrica et Neurologica Scandinavica,* 1959, **34**, 18–25.

CRONHOLM, B., & LAGERGREN, A. Memory disturbances after electroconvulsive therapy. 3. An experimental study of retrograde amnesia after electroconvulsive shock. *Acta Psychiatrica et Neurologica Scandinavica,* 1959, **34**, 283–310.

CRONHOLM, B., & MOLANDER, L. Memory disturbances after electroconvulsive therapy. 1. Conditions 6 hours after electroshock treatment. *Acta Psychiatrica et Neurologica Scandinavica,* 1957, **32**, 280–306.

DAVIDSON, P. O., PAYNE, R. W., & SLOANE, R. B. Cortical inhibition, drive level and conditioning. *Journal of Abnormal Psychology,* 1966, **71**, 310–314.

DESPERT, J. L. Schizophrenia in children. *Psychiatric Quarterly,* 1938, **12**, 366–377.

DIEFENDORF, A. R. *Clinical psychiatry.* New York: Macmillan, 1921.

DOHRENWEND, B. P., & DOHRENWEND, B. S. The problem of validity in field studies of psychological disorder. *Journal of Abnormal Psychology,* 1965, **70**, 52–69.

Dohrenwend, B. S., & Dohrenwend, B. P.   Field studies of social factors in relation to three types of psychological disorder. *Journal of Abnormal Psychology,* 1967, **72,** 369–378.

Dureman, I.   Rate of extinction of a conditioned electrodermal response (EDR) as related to variability of shock intensity during acquisition. *Scandinavian Journal of Psychology,* 1963, 4, 139–142.

Eriksen, C. W., & Browne, T.   An experimental and theoretical analysis of perceptual defense. *Journal of Abnormal and Social Psychology,* 1956, **52,** 224–230.

Escalona, S.   Some considerations regarding psychotherapy with psychotic children. *Bulletin of the Menninger Clinic,* 1948, **12,** 126–134.

Essen-Möller, E.   Individual traits and morbidity in a Swedish rural population. *Acta Psychiatrica et Neurologica Scandinavica,* 1956, **100,** 1–160 (Suppl.).

Eysenck, H. J.   *The dynamics of anxiety and hysteria.* London: Routledge & Kegan Paul, 1957.

Eysenck, H. J.   Classification and the problem of diagnosis. In H. J. Eysenck (Ed.), *Handbook of abnormal psychology.* London: Pitman, 1960. Pp. 1–31.

Eysenck, H. J.   Extraversion and the acquisition of eyeblink and GSR conditioned responses. *Psychological Bulletin,* 1965, **63,** 258–270.

Fitzelle, G. T.   Personality factors and certain attitudes toward child-rearing among parents of asthmatic children. *Psychosomatic Medicine,* 1959, **21,** 208–217.

Fowles, D. C.   Autonomic dysfunction, premorbid adjustment and psychomotor performance in schizophrenia. Unpublished doctoral dissertation, Harvard University, Cambridge, Mass., 1966.

Funkenstein, D. H., Greenblatt, M., Rool, S., & Solomon, H. C.   Psychophysiological study of mentally ill patients. II: Changes in the reactions to epinephrine and mecholyl after electric shock treatment. *American Journal of Psychiatry,* 1949, **106,** 116–121.

Funkenstein, D. H., King, S. H., & Drolette, M.   The experimental evocation of stress. *Symposium on stress.* Army Medical Graduate School, Washington, D. C., 1953.

Garmezy, N.   Stimulus differentiation by schizophrenic and normal subjects under conditions of reward and punishment. *Journal of Personality,* 1952, **20,** 253–276.

Gellhorn, E., & Loofbourrow, G. N.   *Emotions and emotional disorders.* New York: Harper & Row, 1963.

GIBBS, F. A., GIBBS, A. L., & LENNOX, W. G. Electroencephalographic classification of epileptic patients and control subjects. *Archives of Neurology and Psychiatry,* 1943, **50,** 111–128.

GOFFMAN, E. *Asylums.* New York: Doubleday, 1961.

GOSSETT, J. T. An experimental demonstration of Freudian repression proper. Unpublished doctoral dissertation, University of Arkansas, Fayettesville, Ark., 1964.

GOTTESMAN, I. I., & SHIELDS, J. Contribution of twin studies to perspectives in schizophrenia. In B. A. Maher (Ed.), *Progress in experimental personality research. Vol. III.* New York: Academic Press, 1966. Pp. 1–84.

GREGORY, I. Genetic factors in schizophrenia. *American Journal of Psychiatry,* 1960, **116,** 961–972.

GUERTIN, W. H. Empirical syndrome groupings of schizophrenic hospital admissions. *Journal of Clinical Psychology,* 1961, **17,** 268–275.

HALL, K. R. L., & CROOKES, T. G. Studies in learning impairment. II: Psychoneurotics. *Journal of Mental Science,* 1952, **98,** 273–279.

HARRIS, J. G. Size estimation of pictures as a function of thematic content for schizophrenic and normal subjects. *Journal of Personality,* 1957, **25,** 651–671.

HEALY, W., BRONNER, A. F., & BOWERS, A. M. *The structure and meaning of psychoanalysis.* New York: Knopf, 1930.

HEBB, D. O. Alice in Wonderland or psychology among the biological sciences. In H. F. Harlow & C. N. Woolsey (Eds.), *Biological and biochemical bases of behavior.* Madison, Wis.: University of Wisconsin Press, 1958.

HENDRICK, I. *Facts and theories of psychoanalysis.* (3rd ed.). New York: Knopf, 1958.

HESS, E. H., SELTZER, A. L., & SHLIEN, J. M. Pupil response of hetero- and homosexual males to pictures of men and women: A pilot study. *Journal of Abnormal Psychology,* 1965, **70,** 165–168.

HILL, D. Psychiatry. In D. Hill & G. Parr (Eds.), *Electroencephalography.* New York: Macmillan, 1950. Pp. 319–363.

HOCH, P., & ZUBIN, J. (Eds.), *Current problems in psychiatric diagnosis.* New York: Grune & Stratton, 1953.

HOLLINGSHEAD, A. B., & REDLICH, F. C. *Social class and mental illness.* New York: Wiley, 1958.

HOTCHKISS, G. D., CARMAN, L., OGILBY, A. & WIESENFELD, S. Mothers of young male schizophrenic patients as visitors in a mental hospital. *Journal of Nervous and Mental Disease,* 1955, **121**, 452–462.

KAELBLING, R., KING, F. A., ACHENBACH, K., BRANSON, R., & PASAMANICK, B.   Reliability of autonomic responses. *Psychological Reports,* 1960, **6**, 143–163.

KALLMAN, F. J.   The genetic theory of schizophrenia—an analysis of 691 twin index families. *American Journal of Psychiatry,* 1946, **103**, 309–322.

KALLMAN, F. J.   *Genetics of psychosis.* Paris: Hermann, 1950.

KASANIN, J., KNIGHT, E., & SAGE, P.   The parent-child relationship in schizophrenia. *Journal of Nervous and Mental Disease,* 1934, **97**, 249–263.

KRAMER, M., POLLACK, E. S., & REDNICK, R. W.   Studies of the incidence and prevalence of hospitalized mental disorders in the United States: Current status and future goals. In P. H. Hoch & J. Zubin (Eds.), *Comparative epidemiology of the mental disorders.* New York: Grune & Stratton, 1961. Pp. 56–100.

LACEY, J. I., BATEMAN, D. E., & VAN LEHN, R.   Autonomic response specificity. *Psychosomatic Medicine,* 1953, **15**, 10–21.

LACEY, J. I., & SMITH, R. L.   Conditioning and generalization of unconscious anxiety. *Science,* 1954, **120**, 1045–1052.

LANG, P. J., LAZOVIK, A. D., & REYNOLDS, D. J.   Desensitization, suggestibility and pseudotherapy. *Journal of Abnormal Psychology,* 1965, **70**, 395–402.

LEJEUNE, J., TURPIN, R., & GAUTIER, M.   Le mongolism, premier example d'aberration autosomique humaine. *Année Génétique,* 1959, **2**, 41–49.

LEMKAU, P.   *Mental hygiene in public health.* New York: McGraw-Hill, 1949.

LIDZ, T., CORNELISON, A., FLECK, S., & TERRY, D.   The intrafamilial environment of schizophrenic patients. II, marital schism and marital skew. *American Journal of Psychiatry,* 1957, **114**, 241–248.

LIDZ, T., PARKER, B. & CORNELISON, A.   The role of the father in the family environment of the schizophrenic patient. *American Journal of Psychiatry,* 1956, **113**, 126–132.

LIEBNER, D.   Stress in the laboratory and in the natural habitat. A methodological comparison. Unpublished master's thesis. University of Wisconsin, Madison, Wis., 1966.

LINDSLEY, D. B.   Psychophysiology and motivation. In M. R. Jones

(Ed.), *Nebraska symposium on motivation* (pp. 44–105) Lincoln, Nebr.: University of Nebraska Press, 1957.

LINDSLEY, O. R. Characteristics of the behavior of chronic psychotics as revealed by free-operant conditioning methods. *Diseases of the Nervous System: Monog. Supp.*, 1960, **21**, 66–78.

LORAND, S., & FELDMAN, S. The symbolism of teeth in dreams. *International Journal of Psychoanalysis*, 1955, **35**, 145–161.

MAHER, B. A. *Principles of psychopathology.* New York: McGraw-Hill, 1966.

MAHER, B. A., McKEAN, K. O., & McLAUGHLIN, B. Studies in psychotic language. In P. Stone (Ed.), *The general inquirer: A computer approach to content analysis.* Cambridge, Mass.: M.I.T. Press, 1966.

MALMO, R. B. Activation: A neuropsychological dimension. *Psychological Review*, 1959, **66**, 367–386.

MALMO, R. B., & AMSEL, A. Anxiety-produced interference in serial rote learning with observations on rote learning after partial frontal lobectomy. *Journal of Experimental Psychology*, 1949, **38**, 434–440.

MEDNICK, S. A., & SCHULSINGER, F. A longitudinal study of children with a high risk for schizophrenia: A preliminary report. In S. Vandenberg (Ed.), *Methods and goals in human behavior genetics.* New York: Academic Press, 1965.

MEEHL, P. E. Structured and projective tests: Some common problems in validation. *Journal of Projective Techniques*, 1959, **23**, 268–272.

MEHLMAN, B. The reliability of psychiatric diagnosis. *Journal of Abnormal and Social Psychology*, 1952, **47**, 577–578.

METCALFE, M. Demonstration of a psychosomatic relationship. *British Journal of Medical Psychology*, 1956, **29**, 63–66.

MEYER, V. Psychological effects of brain damage. In H. J. Eysenck (Ed.), *Handbook of abnormal psychology.* London: Pitman, 1960. Pp. 529–565.

NAGEL, E. *The structure of science.* New York: Harcourt Brace, 1961.

OSGOOD, C. E., & WALKER, E. Motivation and language behavior: A content analysis of suicide notes. *Journal of Abnormal and Social Psychology*, 1959, **59**, 58–67.

PEASTREL, A. Studies in efficiency: Semantic generalization in schizophrenia. Unpublished doctoral dissertation, University of Pennsylvania, 1961.

PERSONS, R. W., & BRUNING, J. L. Instrumental learning with sociopaths. *Journal of Abnormal Psychology*, 1966, **71**, 165–168.

RAINES, G. N., & ROHRER, J. H.   The operational matrix of psychiatric practice, I: Consistency and variability in interview impressions of different psychiatrists. *American Journal of Psychiatry*, 1955, **110**, 721–733.

RHAN, A.   Erklärungsversuch des Zahnreitztraumes. *Internationale Zeitschrift für Psychoanalyse*, 1932, **18**, 19–20.

ROKEACH, M.   *The Three Christs of Ypsilanti*. New York: Knopf, 1964.

ROSENTHAL, R.   The effect of the experimenter on the results of psychological research. In B. A. Maher (Ed.), *Progress in experimental personality research. Vol. I.* New York: Academic Press, 1964. Pp. 79–114.

ROTH, W. F., & LUTON, F. B.   The mental hygiene program in Tennessee. *American Journal of Psychiatry*, 1943, **99**, 662–675.

SANDIFER, M. G., Jr., PETTUS, C., & QUADE, D.   A study of psychiatric diagnosis. *Journal of Nervous and Mental Disease*, 1964, **139**, 350–356.

SANUA, V. D.   The sociocultural aspects of childhood schizophrenia. In G. H. Zuk & I. Borsomenyi-Nagy (Eds.) *Family therapy and disturbed families.* Palo Alto, Calif.: Science & Behavior Books, 1967. Pp. 159–176.

SARETSKY, T.   The effects of chlorpromazine on primary process thought manifestations. *Journal of Abnormal Psychology*, 1966, **71**, 247–252.

SAUCER, R. T.   A futher study of the perception of apparent motion by schizophrenics. *Journal of Consulting Psychology*, 1958, **22**, 256–258.

SCHACHTER, S., & SINGER, J. E.   Cognitive, social and physiological determinants of emotional state. *Psychological Review*, 1962, **69**, 379–399.

SCHILDER, P.   The psychology of schizophrenia. *Psychoanalytic Review*, 1939, **26**, 380–398.

SCHNEIDMAN, E. S., & FARBEROW, N. L.   Some comparisons between genuine and simulated suicide notes in terms of Mowrer's concepts of discomfort and relief. *Journal of General Psychology*, 1957, **56**, 251–256.

SCHOFIELD, W., & BALIAN, L.   A comparative study of the personal histories of schizophrenic and non-psychiatric patients. *Journal of Abnormal and Social Psychology*, 1959, **59**, 215–225.

SCHOOLER, C., & TECCE, J. J.   Verbal paired-associates learning in chronic schizophrenics as a function of positive and negative evaluation. *Journal of Abnormal Psychology,* 1967, **72,** 151–156.

SCHWAB, P. S. *Electroencephalography in clinical practice.* Philadelphia: Saunders, 1951.

SELYE, H. *The Stress of Life.* London: Longmans, 1957.

SHAGASS, C., NAIMON, J., & MIHALIK, J. An objective test which differentiates between neurotic and psychotic depression. *Archives of Neurology and Psychiatry,* 1956, **75,** 461–471.

SHAGASS, C., & SCHWARTZ, M. Cerebral cortical reactivity in psychotic depressions. *Archives of General Psychiatry,* 1962, **6,** 235–242.

SHIELDS, J., & SLATER, E. Heredity and psychological abnormality. In H. J. Eysenck (Ed.), *Handbook of abnormal psychology.* London: Pitman, 1960. Pp. 298–343.

SLATER, E. Diagnosis of zygosity by fingerprints. *Acta Psychiatrica Scandinavia,* 1963, **39,** 78–84.

SOLOMON, R. L., & POSTMAN, L. E. Frequency of usages as a determinant of recognition thresholds for words. *Journal of Experimental Psychology,* 1952, **43,** 195–201.

SPENCE, K. W. A theory of emotionally based drive (D) and its relation to performance in simple learning situations. *American Psychologist,* 1958, **13,** 131–141.

SPIEGEL, D. E., & NEURINGER, C. Role of dread in suicidal behavior. *Journal of Abnormal and Social Psychology,* 1963, **66,** 507–511.

STERN, C. *Principles of human genetics.* (2nd ed.). San Francisco: Freeman, 1960.

STRÖMGREN, E. Zum Ersatz des Weinbergschen "abgekürtzen Verfahrens," zugleich ein Beitrag zur Frage von der Erblichkeit des Erkrankungsalters bei der Schizophrenie. *Zeitschrift für die gesamte Neurologie und Psychiatrie,* 1935, **153,** 789–797.

TIETZE, T. A study of mothers of schizophrenic patients. *Psychiatry,* 1949, **12,** 55–65.

TIZARD, J., & VENABLES, P. H. The influence of extraneous stimulation on the reaction time of schizophrenics. *British Journal of Psychology,* 1957, **48,** 299–305.

THOMAS, D. R., & KONICK, D. S. A comparison of different measures of response strength in the study of stimulus generalization. *Journal of the experimental analysis of behavior,* 1966, **9,** 239–242.

VENABLES, P. H. Input dysfunction in schizophrenia. In B. A. Maher

(Ed.), *Progress in experimental personality research, Vol. I.* New York: Academic Press, 1964.

VERPLANCK, W. S.   A glossary of some terms used in the objective science of behavior. *Psychological Review,* 1957, **64,** Suppl.

WEBB, E. J., CAMPBELL, D. T., SCHWARTZ, R. D., & SECHREST, L. *Unobtrusive measures: nonreactive research in the social sciences.* Chicago: Rand McNally, 1966.

WEINBERG, W.   Beiträge zur Physiologie und Pathologie der Mehrlingsgeburten beim Menschen. *Archive für gesamte Physiologie,* 1901, **38,** 346–430.

WEINER, H., THALER, M., REISER, M. F., & MIRSKY, I. A.   Etiology of duodenal ulcer, I. Relation of specific psychological characteristics to rate of gastric secretion (serum pepsinogen). *Psychosomatic Medicine.* 1957, **19,** 1–10.

WENGER, M. A., JONES, F. N., & JONES, M. H.   *Physiological Psychology.* New York: Holt, Rinehart & Winston, 1956.

WHITE, R. W.   *The abnormal personality.* (2nd ed.). New York: Ronald Press, 1956.

WILLIAMS, E. B.   Deductive reasoning in schizophrenia. *Journal of Abnormal and Social Psychology,* 1964, **69,** 47–61.

WISHNER, J.   The concept of efficiency in psychological health and psychopathology. *Psychological Review,* 1955, **62,** 69–80.

WITTENBORN, J. R.   The dimensions of psychosis. *Journal of Nervous and Mental Disease,* 1962, **134,** 117–128.

WOLFF, C.   *A psychology of gesture.* London: Methuen, 1948.

ZIGLER, E., & PHILLIPS, L.   Psychiatric diagnosis: A critique. *Journal of Abnormal and Social Psychology,* 1961, **3,** 607–618.

ZIMMERMAN, C., & BAUER, R. A.   The influence of an audience on what is remembered. *Public Opinion Quarterly,* 1956, **20,** 238–248.

GLOSSARY

Addiction: A habit, particularly that of taking certain drugs, which is dangerous to health and difficult to extinguish. Termination of the habit may lead to bodily changes, termed "withdrawal symptoms."

Amnesia: Loss of memory for a particular period of one's life; amnesia occurs suddenly and may last for a few days or for many years.

Anesthesia: Loss of sensitivity to stimuli, whether because of use of a drug, neural lesions, or functional disorder. It may be local or general.

Anesthesia, glove, shoe, or stocking: Insensitivity to touch in the area indicated. It is demonstrably a symptom of a functional disorder, generally hysteria, and does not correspond with the neurological substrate of touch sensation.

Asthma: A disease characterized by difficulty of breathing, accompanied by a wheezing sound, a sense of constriction in the chest, a cough, and expectoration. It may or may not have a psychological component in its etiology.

Colitis: Inflammation of the large intestine, especially of its mucous membrane. It may or may not have psychological component in its etiology.

Compulsion: An irrational, repetitive act generally classified as neurotic. Performance of the act appears to be reinforced by anxiety reduction.

Conduct disorder: Disorders of behavior in which the chief component is antisocial action and in which there is little or no evidence of neurotic anxiety.

Confounding: 1. To combine data from separate sources of variation into a single measure.

2. To design an experiment in such a way that the independent variable is inadvertently correlated with an undesired source of variance, e.g., when selecting for cerebroarteriosclerosis it is difficult to avoid confounding this disorder with the factor of old age.

Control group: Persons who are not exposed to the experimental variable but are exposed to as many as possible (and ideally all) of the other conditions in the experiment in order to ensure that the effects of the experiment are not the result of irrelevant or unnoticed considerations.

Criterion measure: A score in the dependent variable, in the variable to be predicted, or in the variable that serves as a criterion.

Data: The raw material of observation, or any number quantities derived from them before inference has taken place.

Depression: A state of great sadness, often accompanied by guilt and anxiety, gloomy ruminations, apathetic fatigue, inability to respond to pleasant stimuli, suicidal impulses, sleeplessness, and feelings of worthlessness.

Discriminant validity: The power of a measurement procedure to distinguish the presence of a particular variable from among others contributing to a complex phenomenon.

ECT: (Electroconvulsive therapy) a technique of somatic treatment in which there is passage of electric current through the frontal area of the patient's head. Most commonly used in the depressions.

Etiology: Origins or causes, especially of a disease.

Euphoria: An emotional condition wherein the patient experiences a feeling of well-being.

Factor-analysis: A statistical method for analyzing scores and correlations between scores from a number of tests so as to produce a number of explanatory factors.

GSR: (Galvanic skin response) electrical reactions of the skin, related to perspiration, measured by a galvanometer.

Gaussian curve: Normal curve, following a frequency distribution characterized by the bell-shaped curve.

Generalization: The transfer of responses acquired from one stimulus configuration to others that have some similarity to it.

Hives (urticaria): An eruptive skin disease.

Huntington's chorea: A degenerative disorder of the nervous system of apparent genetic origin.

Hyper-: A prefix (e.g., *hyper*active) meaning excessive or of unusual magnitude.

Hypo-: A prefix meaning below, under, defective, lacking (e.g., *hypo*thyroidism: insufficiency of thyroid function).

Hypothesis: A tentative interpretation of a set of data, the explanation usually specifying some theoretical relationship.

Hysteria: A pattern of neurotic behavior disorder in which denial of some aspect of reality is central, e.g., hysterical blindness, loss of memory. A wide range of symptoms is possible.

Hysterical: Of symptoms due to a basic disorder of hysteria.

Manifest Anxiety Scale (Taylor MAS): A questionnaire that measures general anxiety or generalized "arousal."

Mannerism: A personal peculiarity of speech or behavior.

Obsession: An irrational, repetitive thought.

Peptic ulcer: An ulcer connected with or caused by digestive juices. It may or may not have psychological components in its etiology.

Perceptual constancy: The tendency for stimulus objects to be perceived in terms of their "typical" or standard appearance even when local variations in conditions have changed their object qualities.

Phobia: Any extreme, irrational fear.

Placebo: An inert or inactive treatment (especially used in drug studies) which is given to the patient with the suggestion that it is a medication, and which permits comparison with the effects of active treatment.

Precipitating: A factor which, added to preexisting factors, produces an overt result, e.g., loss of employment may precipitate depression in a predisposed individual.

Premorbid: The state existing in a patient's life prior to the appearance of pathology.

Prognosis: An estimate of the future course of a disorder, including probability of recovery.

Psychoanalyst: A psychotherapist who follows the therapeutic procedures and principles advocated by Freud, including later developments.

Psychometric test: Any quantitative assessment of an individual's psychological traits or attributes.

Psychopathy: A disorder including antisocial behavior with indifference to the consequences, absence of guilt and inability to form close personal attachments.

Recidivism: The repetition or recurrence of a criminal act.

Repeat reliability: The extent to which a measure will produce the same result when applied to the same phenomenon a second time.

Schizoid: Refers to behavior characterized by withdrawal, poor reality contact, and other schizophrenic symptoms. Schizoid personality is often used to refer to the premorbid personality of the schizophrenic patient.

Schizophrenia: A group of disorders characterized by perceptual distortion, emotional disturbance, and serious deviance of intellectual, verbal, and motor behavior.

Sensitivity: The extent to which a measurement procedure responds to small changes in the attributes it is intended to measure.

Significance (statistical): The probability that a given set of data would occur by random sampling from a specified population. Conventionally, where this is 5 percent or less, the data are said to be significantly different from chance.

Syndrome: A pattern of symptoms.

Test-retest reliability: A stability coefficient which answers the question: If the same test is given again, after a suitable interval to minimize differential practice effects, will comparable scores be obtained?

Variable, dependent and independent: Dependent variable: a variable whose changes are treated as being consequent upon changes in one or more other variables, called collectively the independent variable. In psychology the measured dependent value is always the response.

Independent variable: the variable whose changes are regarded as not dependent upon changes in another specified variable; the variable which is manipulated or treated in an experiment to see what effect changes in that variable bring about in the variables regarded as dependent on it. The independence asserted is not absolute.

White noise: Random fluctuation noise; the noise that is heard when very many sound waves of different lengths are combined so that they reinforce or cancel one another in a haphazard fashion.

Indexes

Name Index

Subject Index